MENDING A
FRACTURED CHURCH

How to Seek Unity with Integrity

MENDING A FRACTURED CHURCH

How to Seek Unity with Integrity

EDITED BY MICHAEL BIRD AND BRIAN ROSNER

LEXHAM PRESS

Mending a Fractured Church: How to Seek Unity with Integrity

Copyright 2015 Lexham Press

Lexham Press, 1313 Commercial St., Bellingham, WA 98225
LexhamPress.com

Unless otherwise noted, Scripture quotations are the author's own
translation.

Scripture quotations marked (ASV) are from the American Standard
Version. Public domain.

Scripture quotations marked (ESV) are from ESV® Bible (The Holy Bible,
English Standard Version®), copyright © 2001 by Crossway Bibles, a
publishing ministry of Good News Publishers. Used by permission. All
rights reserved.

Scripture quotations marked (HCSB) are from the Holman Christian
Standard Bible®, Copyright © 1999, 2000, 2002, 2003, 2009 by Holman
Bible Publishers. Used by permission. Holman Christian Standard
Bible®, Holman CSB®, and HCSB® are federally registered trademarks of
Holman Bible Publishers.

Scripture quotations marked (LEB) are from the Lexham English Bible,
copyright 2013 by Lexham Press. Lexham is a registered trademark of
Faithlife Corporation.

Scripture quotations marked (NIV) are from the Holy Bible, NEW
INTERNATIONAL VERSION®. Copyright © 1973, 1978, 1984 by Biblica,
Inc. Used by permission. All rights reserved worldwide.

Scripture quotations marked (NRSV) are from the New Revised Standard
Version Bible, copyright © 1989, National Council of the Churches of
Christ in the United States of America. Used by permission. All rights
reserved.

Scripture quotations marked (KJV) are from the King James Version.
Public domain.

Print ISBN 9781577996316
Digital ISBN 9781577996866

Lexham Editorial Team: Rebecca Brant, Lynnea Fraser
Cover Design: Christine Gerhart
Typesetting: ProjectLuz.com

CONTENTS

FOREWORD

Graham Cole

When Christians disagree, how may the bonds of peace be preserved? It is so good to see an interdisciplinary approach to the question. Lindsay Wilson works in the field of the Old Testament, Brian Rosner in the New Testament, Andrew Malone in both as well as mission, Mike Bird in systematic theology, and Rhys Bezzant in church history. Lindsay Wilson tackles a key Old Testament passage (Josh 22:1–34) and Brian Rosner an New Testament one (Rom 14:1–15:7). Mike Bird offers a theological reflection on when Christians divide. Rhys Bezzant looks at relevant Protestant history on the subject. Andrew Malone sets up the discussion. They wear their scholarship lightly.

It was the Lutheran Rupertus Meldenius (1582–1651) who reputedly said: "In the essentials unity, in the non-essentials or doubtful things liberty, and in all things charity." The three categories are so useful, but the question is what goes into each. This very helpful work, by five scholars based at Ridley College, Melbourne, assists us in navigating the way forward.

PREFACE

Brian Rosner

When the Christians in Rome were squabbling over what the Apostle Paul called "disputable matters," he summed up his advice to them in this way: "Let us pursue what makes for peace and for mutual upbuilding." The implication is clear; to behave badly in such circumstances will lead to strife and demolish the church. It will also impede the progress of the gospel. Like it or not, the reputation of God and the gospel are tied to the behavior of his people.

When I became principal of Ridley College in 2012 it quickly became clear to me that Melbourne was a context in which knowing how to deal with disputable matters was an essential requirement for my work. However, finding an approach to such matters—one that did not compromise the gospel and was more than merely pragmatic—was not easy. Recognizing my own inadequacy, I turned to my colleagues.

On September 2, 2013, we held a daylong Ridley Pastoral Seminar on the subject of disputable matters. Five members of the faculty were involved, including me. We approached the topic from the different angles of our various disciplines. Indeed, in addressing something of such practical import, both the Old Testament and New Testament, along with systematic theology and church history, have important things to say. This little book grew out of that conference.

Too often questions of church unity are decided with little theological reflection and without due attention to the whole counsel of God in Scripture. Our responses to those with whom we differ regularly arise without reflection from our experiences, personalities, and social settings, or from a few convenient proof texts. Such responses do much damage to individuals and churches. Our hope and prayer is that this slim volume will contribute to an approach that is more biblical and more theological, based on the conviction that only such an approach will lead to unity with integrity.

INTRODUCTION

Michael Bird and Brian Rosner

Southern Baptist theologian Timothy George asks the highly provocative question,

> When Jesus said, "Upon this rock I will build my church, and the gates of hell shall not prevail against it," did he intend that the people called to bear his name in the world would eventually be divided into 37,000 competing denominations? That is the number of separate Christian bodies worldwide, according to missions statistician Todd Johnson of the World Christian Database. ... Sometimes church division is a tragic necessity, and the call to Christian unity does not mean that we must blend all believers into a single homogenous unity. But neither does it allow us to relax and accept the status quo as God's perfect will.[1]

George makes a very good point. Christian churches, especially Protestants, are hopelessly divided and notoriously good at dividing. Sometimes these divisions have been triggered by seismic debates over major

---

1. Timothy George, "Is Christ Divided?" *Christianity Today* 49, no. 7 (2005): 31.

doctrines within the Christian faith about the nature of God, the gift of salvation, and the very meaning of the gospel. However, other debates, which can fracture fellowship and sprout entirely new denominations, are over matters that are clearly secondary. The tragedy is not only that the churches are fractured but that they are fractured over matters when they need not be. The editors of this volume do not contest the need to take decisive and potentially divisive actions when the gospel is threatened by those who have acceded to a blatantly heterodox version of the Christian faith. However, we do lament that most congregational divisions are not over primary issues and pertain instead to secondary or even tertiary subjects. In sum, we feel that churches need more than ever to heed the Apostle Paul's charge to accept one another "without quarreling over disputable matters" (Rom 14:1 NIV). That is the theme of this volume.

We are not so glib as to suppose that all divisions can be ended by simply reading a couple of Bible verses, offering a hearty handshake, and sharing a casserole at a church potluck. The obvious problem is to determine what matters that can cause schism are beyond dispute, and what are the disputable matters that we are at liberty to dispute within the bounds of Christian fellowship. In other words, what we need to develop is a theological triage in relation to (1) views *essential* to the faith, (2) views *important* to the faith and order of a church but not necessary for salvation, and (3) views that may be treated with *indifference*, a matter of conscience, often called *adiaphora*.[2] Most of us will be able to agree on the primary matters like the Trinity, Jesus' atoning death, his bodily resurrection, salvation by grace alone, and the return of the Lord Jesus. We might even be able to agree on secondary matters like baptism and church governance. We might be able to agree as to what is a tertiary matter, like whether Christians should drink alcohol, what Bible translation we should use, or whether we should fast. The real problem is how we can disagree over secondary and tertiary matters without breaking the bonds of Christian fellowship. That is the real challenge for many churches.

As a preliminary piece of advice, we would say that the New Testament, particularly 1 Corinthians 8 and Romans 14, contains several helpful principles that we should apply to disputable matters that might arise in our churches.[3]

1. Learn to differentiate between areas of conviction and areas of command.

2. Don't major on minor doctrines or minor on majors.

3. Withhold judgment where the gospel is not threatened and holiness is not compromised.

4. Exercise your convictions to build others up, not to tear them down.

---

2. Cf. Albert Mohler, "A Call for Theological Triage and Christian Maturity," July 12, 2015, www.albertmohler.com/2005/07/12/a-call-for-theological-triage-and-christian-maturity/.

3. Michael F. Bird, *Bird's-Eye View of Paul* (Nottingham, UK: Inter-Varsity Press, 2008), 154.

5.   Do not exchange freedom in Christ for slavery to human tradition.

6.   At all times act in love and carry each other's burdens.

We believe that following the checklist above is how we can "make every effort to do what leads to peace and to mutual edification" (Rom 14:19 NIV). The underlying principle, as many have said before, is "In the essentials unity, in the non-essentials liberty, but in all things charity."

It is along these lines that the various contributors to this volume present their own studies about how to deal with disputable matters within Christian churches. The aim is not to stifle debate through a corny appeal to unity. Rather, the objective is to recognize that there are differences of opinion among our brothers and sisters over topics that matter to many of us and carry the weight of people's convictions and consciences. However, at the end of the day, we are prepared to argue that the big things uniting us are infinitely more powerful than any of the smaller things that might divide us. Therefore, our aim is to provide exegetical bulk, theological perspective, and pastoral counsel about how to survive disputes over disputable matters and to stop churches from fracturing.

Andrew Malone begins the volume by pointing out that we need to determine when a matter is of secondary importance and then proceed to navigate that dispute graciously. However, the existence of secondary matters should not lead us to presume blithely that any and every difference between believers is of a secondary nature and should be tolerated. As this volume comes to explore just how some disputes might be managed, Malone says that we need to appreciate the weight that Scripture places on unity among God's people. Consequently, his essay looks at how highly unity is valued, the recognition that some diversity can and should exist within the body of Christ, and the great weight placed on humility. Malone surmises that the biblical authors are as much interested in pastoral harmony and self-sacrificial compromise as in the rigid defense of theologically superior accuracy.

Lindsay Wilson argues that the Old Testament is a neglected resource in dealing with disputes between believers. While the Old Testament contains many examples of conflicts resolved (e.g., Jacob and Esau; Joseph and his brothers; David, Abigail, and Nabal), the story of the Transjordanian and other tribes in Joshua 22 stands out because it deals with two groups that have a right motivation for their actions. The intent of the Transjordanian tribes was to witness to their unity with the rest of Israel, while the intent of other tribes was to stand up for God's honor, which they thought was compromised by the building of an altar. Wilson explores the story of Joshua 22 and draws out a number of key principles: not letting differences divide, the importance of facing up to conflict, devoting one's best resources to conflict resolution, and the pivotal role of a generous spirit.

Brian Rosner examines Romans 14–15 as a case study of disputable matters. In a patient teasing out of the dynamics of the dispute and Paul's response, Rosner observes that Paul stresses the need for personal convictions, flexibility, not judging or despising those who disagree, and the goal of peace and edification. Further, he notices that the theological foundations of Paul's teaching on disputable matters are remarkably profound. Doctrine matters, especially when it comes to disputable matters. Paul appeals to the lordship of Christ, the imitation of Christ, justification by faith, and the work of the Spirit in the kingdom of God. There is indeed much at stake: To behave badly will damage the health and happiness of the church, impede the progress of the gospel, and diminish the glory of God.

Michael Bird surveys the Johannine epistles with a particular focus on their teaching about fellowship and division. Bird notes that the Johannine letters place a huge amount of weight on the theme of love, and remaining in fellowship with other believers is among the chief ways that believers express their love for one another. Even so, Bird also points out that John the Elder regards the church's witness to Jesus as the Messiah and Son of God, including his incarnation and atonement, as a nonnegotiable element of its faith. Indeed, there can be no unity apart from a shared profession of a common faith in Jesus as the Son. According to Bird, John is brutally honest that division can arise when dissent about the nature and identity of Jesus ferments within a fellowship, and the proper response to such dissent is either discipline or expulsion. It would seem, Bird concludes, that John believes in the imperatives of love and unity, and yet never at the expense of the christological foundations of the church. When someone unwisely attempts to demolish those foundations, schism may in fact be the inevitable result.

From a historical perspective, Rhys Bezzant investigates the development of thinking concerning disputable matters among Protestants from the sixteenth century until today. While Luther focused on the core of the gospel to leverage reform, Calvin explained both center and perimeter theologically. The Anglican Reformers created some measure of church uniformity, while at the same time building assumptions concerning primary and secondary teachings into their formularies. North American Puritans, on the other hand, subjected true faith to true order, making the purity of the gospel dependent on the structure of the church preaching it. The evangelical revival of the eighteenth century highlighted a new criterion for distinguishing first- and second-order issues, namely the reality of regeneration, or visible vital piety, making their ministry priorities contextually responsive. Global missions, the ecumenical movement, and disputes within the Anglican Communion suggest the value of affirming the place of disputable matters in the church today.

Such studies, we hope, will equip seminary students, ministers, and church leaders to consider how to pursue the unity of a church while holding to the "first things" of faith. In other words, the volume is a call to *not* major on the minors *or* to minor on the majors. Instead, we need to pursue corporate unity with theological integrity.

CHAPTER 1

DISPUTABLE MATTERS

Constraining the Topic

Andrew S. Malone

INTRODUCTION

Christians disagree. We even disagree about how to disagree, hence this volume. Moreover, many of us tend to polarize when a contentious issue arises. Baptism of infants versus the baptism of inherently older believers. Tolerance of alcohol versus prohibition. Black versus white. Me versus you.

Both church history and our contemporary experience verify that many thorny issues are not resolved through such polarization. I was struck recently by a helpful example of balance. Considering the evidence for the Holy Spirit in the Old Testament, David Firth overtly maps out the opposite extremes toward which interpreters trend: to minimize any hints and find nothing of the Spirit, or to maximize every possible hint and virtually discern a full-blown revelation of the

Trinity. His short survey seeks a middle path between both extremes.[1]

As we approach the topic of Christians differing among themselves, the remaining contributions in this collection explore the mechanics of differing. There seem to be several clear examples among the earliest believers where major disagreements, at least over secondary matters, were identified and tolerated. Both Jews and Gentiles became followers of Jesus, but they did not share a uniform approach to matters of religious observance like diet. Even within these broad religious boundaries we find subdivisions, such as believing Jews in Jerusalem who had a Hebrew-speaking background and those who had a Greek-speaking background (Acts 6:1–6).

Given the tendency of my colleagues to explore the permissibility or overcoming of differences, my opening contribution reminds us that this tendency does not grant us carte blanche to differ over everything. We regularly refer to the notion of agreeing over "first-order issues" with liberty to disagree over "second-order matters." All this does is shift questions about permissibility to a different plane: Which issues do we determine to be the nonnegotiable, primary ones, and which can we discern as less prescribed, secondary concerns?

Another way of viewing my immediate purpose is to remind us that not all matters can be classified as secondary. Being allowed to differ over *some* issues does not

---

1. David G. Firth, "God's Spirit in the Old Testament," in *Holy Spirit: Unfinished Agenda*, ed. Johnson T. K. Lim (Singapore: Genesis/Word N Works, 2014), 32–35.

permit us to extend the notion such that we may differ over *all* issues. Biblical teaching remains surprisingly clear about the need for unity and even for uniformity over many central tenets. We are not at liberty to differ over everything. Indeed, in our haste to rationalize our personal preferences and delineate our distinctives, we must be cautious not to transgress a strong call to unified Christian identity.

The remainder of this introductory essay proceeds through three steps. First, we observe the strength of the call to unity—a call that constrains the extremes of liberty for which some may strive. Second, we briefly recognize the kinds of diversity that are explicated elsewhere in Scripture and in this volume. Third, we touch on some of the biblical expectations for navigating matters of diversity without breaching unity.

THE EXPECTATION: UNITY MATTERS

Many of us want to define ourselves by our distinctives. In our race to make ourselves or our local churches distinct from and even competitive with others, we can prioritize those elements of Scripture that condone disagreement. We will survey such passages in due course.

But, first, there is a substantial expectation in Scripture that Christians will aspire to widespread unity. We can sometimes overlook or undersell this aspiration. A survey of some key texts reminds us of the gravity of this expectation. We dare not consider *whether* we may differ and *how* we should differ until we appreciate the divinely mandated momentum that such disagreement resists.

The Old Testament

Although I will not focus on the Old Testament, we will certainly find indicators of unity there.

While various skeptics argue over the purpose of the Old Testament law code, at the very least it is agreed to be a way of distinguishing the people of God from outsiders. Adherence brands the Israelites with a particular identity, demarcated from the other nations around them. God's covenant people are those who uniformly submit to his mandated expectations. The other nations will recognize that there is something distinctive about Israel (e.g., Deut 4:5–8; 28:9–10).[2]

Several of God's expectations are themselves directly concerned with unity. Harmony is a key goal, and there are instructions about how to deal with dissension. This even extends to ensuring that outsiders who join Israel are properly integrated; we read several times that "the same law applies both to the native-born and to the foreigner residing among you" (Exod 12:49 NIV). It is not insignificant that the instance of the instruction cited here comes immediately after "an ethnically diverse crowd" joins Israel in the exodus from Egypt (Exod 12:38 HCSB) as they come to celebrate the first Passover. We are familiar with other famous individuals—Rahab, Ruth, Naaman—who choose to identify themselves with the people of God.[3]

---

2. Christopher J. H. Wright, *The Mission of God: Unlocking the Bible's Grand Narrative* (Nottingham, UK: Inter-Varsity Press, 2006), chaps. 7, 11.

3. Frank Anthony Spina, *The Faith of the Outsider: Exclusion and Inclusion in the Biblical Story* (Grand Rapids: Eerdmans, 2005).

Steps in the opposite direction elicit angst and narratorial disapproval as individuals refuse to conform, as the twelve tribes turn on each other in Judges, and as the united nation splinters into two kingdoms after Solomon. We find some of the later prophets earnestly promising that God might yet reunite what is left of his fragmented people and that he will implant a new heart to enable covenant compliance. The same sentiment is expressed in other writings of the Old Testament. One of the better-known lines from the Psalms reads, "How good and pleasant it is when God's people live together in unity!" (Psa 133:1 NIV). Much in the Wisdom literature instructs about maintaining harmony in various spheres of life.

The Gospels

When we turn to the New Testament, we find abundant testimony about the need for unity among believers. Again, I suspect that rampant Western individualism might blind us to the repetition and strength of such instructions. Even a brief sampling across the New Testament reminds us of a divine distaste for divisions and dissension.

An obvious starting point is the teaching of Jesus. As he closes his famous "high priestly prayer" on the night he was betrayed, he is absolutely adamant that unity among future generations of believers is crucial:

> I ask not only on behalf of these [disciples, whom you gave me from the world], but also on behalf of those who will believe in me through their word, *that they may all be one*. As you, Father, are in me

and I am in you, may they also be in us, so that the world may believe that you have sent me. The glory that you have given me I have given them, *so that they may be one, as we are one,* I in them and you in me, that they may become *completely one,* so that the world may know that you have sent me and have loved them even as you have loved me (John 17:20–23 NRSV).

The import of the repetition is unavoidable. Jesus expects that his followers, even beyond the first generation, will be united. Jesus not only *wants* this, he fervently *prays* that this will be so. And his purpose in this is also clear—and close to evangelical hearts: Jesus' followers need to be "one" so that the world may believe the truth about the Father sending the Son. Put simply, Jesus says both here and elsewhere that you cannot be a Christian believer unless you recognize the central witness afforded by unity.

Acts

We find the same when we move into the biblical narrative of the first decades of the church. We certainly find a string of terms and summaries that confirm the church's unity. Luke outlines a series of impediments to the gospel, and internal disagreements are just as threatening as external opposition. These disagreements threaten to splinter and smother the fledgling church, such as the imbalanced treatment of different ethnic groups (Acts 6:1–7), resistance to the gospel spreading to Gentiles like Cornelius (Acts 11:1–18), and the demand from Christians with a Pharisaic background that all believers must obey the Jewish law (Acts 15:1–21). Yet each impediment to the spread of the gospel is negotiated safely. Indeed, we are not left merely to infer that everyone returns to getting along well; Luke expressly commends this through overt terms of unity and agreement.[4] Much of the friction is concerned with more than mere "disputable," second-order issues. Luke presents us with an ideal of unity in the gospel that we must not disregard.

Paul

The same demand for unity is equally clear in the letters of Paul. One Pauline scholar puts unity at the very core of the church's identity: "For Paul, what differentiated the church from the world was the unity of its members, because society was characterized above all by divisions."[5] Although we trace the idea of unity through Paul's writings in more detail below, here we can capture his key points in just a few images and passages.

In many of his letters Paul returns to the "body" metaphor. Believers have been "reconciled" to God, who has "made peace" with them through the cross (e.g., Col 1:20). In turn, these believers are adopted into a single family and are being knit together into a single body (e.g., Eph 4:15–16). In language that some traditions repeat as

---

4. Alan J. Thompson, "Unity in Acts: Idealization or Reality?," *Journal of the Evangelical Theological Society* 51 (2008): 523–42, especially his opening survey.

5. Jerome Murphy-O'Connor, "Divisions Are Necessary (1 Corinthians 11:19)," in *Celebrating Paul*, ed. Peter Spitaler, Catholic Biblical Quarterly Monograph Series 48 (Washington, DC: Catholic Biblical Association of America, 2011), 9.

a regular part of communion liturgy, Paul spells it out quite clearly: "Because there is one bread, we who are many are one body, for we all partake of the one bread" (1 Cor 10:17 NRSV).[6]

Such imagery coincides again in a famous verse, often invoked when unity needs to be bolstered. "There is no longer Jew or Greek, there is no longer slave or free, there is no longer male and female"—with the reason given—"for all of you are one in Christ Jesus" (Gal 3:28 NRSV). Again, Paul links such unity with family imagery and a sacramental basis; faith in Jesus makes all believers "sons" of God (Gal 3:26), and previous divisions are dispensed with because every believer is baptized into Christ (Gal 3:27).[7]

So Paul has a strong theological foundation when he calls for church unity. Indeed, each letter that emphasizes this body imagery does so as part of an express call to unity. Romans, Galatians, and Ephesians strive to show that differences between Jews and Gentiles are now of secondary importance; 1 Corinthians challenges divisions along other lines. In doing so, Paul seeks to patch up "schisms" and calls for "peace" and the "(re)establishing" of relationships. He regularly uses a short phrase to refer to "the same thing" that believers should think or to which they should aspire.

---

6. Note how "unity" language permeates the analysis of Ronald Y. K. Fung, "Body of Christ," in *Dictionary of Paul and His Letters*, ed. Gerald F. Hawthorne and Ralph P. Martin (Downers Grove, IL: InterVarsity Press, 1993), 76–82.

7. Ben Witherington III, *Grace in Galatia* (Grand Rapids: Eerdmans, 1998), 280, thinks Paul's shaping of the word "one" here invokes again the body metaphor: "all *one united person* in Christ Jesus."

Rather than analyze each term exhaustively, we get an adequate taste of the apostle's goal by seeing how these are regularly collocated in a few important passages on unity.

Brian Rosner's contribution walks us through Romans 14–15 in some detail. At the end of Paul's argument, he prays for the strong and the weak who are struggling: "May the God of endurance and encouragement grant you *to think the same* among one another according to Christ Jesus, in order that, *unanimously*, with *one* mouth/voice you might glorify the God and Father of our Lord Jesus Christ" (Rom 15:5–6).

Just one chapter later, we find a similar sentiment in the opening barrage of 1 Corinthians. Here Paul is dealing with "factions" and "divisions" as various groups in the church side with one apostle or another. Paul's response is familiar to us: "I urge you ... that you all should say *the same* and there should not be divisions among you but that you should be *(re)unified* in *the same mind* and in *the same thought/purpose*" (1 Cor 1:10). The schisms in Corinth are not first-order doctrinal problems but have to do more with allegiances and tribal distinctions within orthodoxy; Paul calls the Corinthians, almost literally, to patch up such minor fractures before they fester.[8]

We move from the opening chapter of 1 Corinthians to the last verses of 2 Corinthians. Before Paul closes with

---

8. "To be 'united' or 'restored' was a surgical term for setting bones and was aptly used as a metaphor for 'resetting' broken relationships and reconciling factions" (Roy E. Ciampa and Brian S. Rosner, *The First Letter to the Corinthians*, Pillar New Testament Commentaries [Grand Rapids: Eerdmans, 2010], 76; see also 81–82).

a command for mutual greeting and what we now call "The Grace," there is another such series of calls for unity. "Finally, brothers and sisters, rejoice, *be (re)unified*, be encouraged, *think the same, be peaceable*, and the God of love and *peace* will be with you" (2 Cor 13:11).

In all this, I do not detect Paul pushing for an unrealistic uniformity. The apostle is not necessarily offended by the existence of differences but by such preferences being expressed in aggressive and competitive fashions. We should also note that Corinth was renowned for its smorgasbord of competing philosophical options. For the believers in that city to perpetuate such one-upmanship did nothing to elevate Christianity beyond any other alternative worldview.

Similar juxtaposition of terms can be found elsewhere in Paul's writings (e.g., Rom 12:16–18; Phil 2:1–2). And there are other terms, like "fellowship" or "partnership," that we have not explored here (and which are also sometimes collocated with the language already surveyed). It is abundantly obvious that Paul thinks highly of church unity. Moreover, he thinks unity is something that is volitional; it is under the control of believers, and they can directly contribute toward it. Paul does expect a degree of conformity that borders on anathema to contemporary individualism. The stark assessment of such passages given in a dictionary from a more conformist generation and a more conformist culture may thus grate on modern ears: "The fundamental demand of Pauline exhortation is a uniform direction, a common mind, and unity of thought and will."[9]

Beyond Paul's Letters

Space precludes study beyond Paul, the primary contributor to the latter half of the New Testament. But we ought not to presume that the remaining letters are silent on these matters, even though themes of unity are not necessarily as prominent there. We might simply note similar instructions in passages like this one of Peter: "To sum up, all of you must be *same-minded*, sympathetic, brother-loving, compassionate, humble-minded ... for to this you were called" (1 Pet 3:8–9). Commentators here regularly show that Peter's special term is the equivalent of Paul's commands to "think the same" and reflects "the quality of harmony within the Christian community highly prized and recommended."[10] Similar concern for unity is found in the letters of John. The call to unity based on the church's identity is also found in the first generation of Christian writers after the New Testament. First- and second-century

---

9. Georg Bertram, "φρήν, κτλ.," in *Theological Dictionary of the New Testament*, ed. Gerhard Friedrich (Grand Rapids: Eerdmans, 1973), 9:233.

10. Paul J. Achtemeier, *1 Peter*, Hermeneia (Minneapolis: Fortress, 1996), 222; cf. J. Ramsey Michaels, *1 Peter*, Word Biblical Commentary 49 (Waco, TX: Word, 1988), 174, 176. Scholars recognize the term is concerned with unity in purpose rather than strict uniformity in every thought.

leaders like Clement and Ignatius continue to propagate what we have already seen.[11]

THE REALITY: DIFFERENCES EXIST

Even our brief survey has reiterated the strength and breadth of the Bible's call to unity. How then should we perceive contemporary disagreements? Does dissonance in our own congregations suggest disobedience to Scripture? The New Testament is clearly in favor of unity and the smoothing over of differences. Yet the New Testament is not ignorant of the possibility of disunity, and it is this recognition that elicits the volume before us.

I still think that there is a general tendency to try to justify or rationalize our differences. Where there are differences within our congregations, and certainly differences between our local church and the next one, we like to think that the Bible permits or perhaps even encourages such distinctions. We may well want to ensure that these differences are not exacerbated to the point of hostile and ungodly competition, yet we still want to gauge how much distinctiveness might be tolerated. Is there some boundary, one side of which we are guilty of disunity but the other side of which we are praised for preserving Christian or denominational purity?

---

11. For examples, see §§8.1–8.3 of Kevin N. Giles, "Church," in *Dictionary of the Later New Testament and Its Developments*, ed. Ralph P. Martin and Peter H. Davids (Downers Grove, IL: InterVarsity Press, 1997), 194–204. The emphasis of Clement and Ignatius on unity is affirmed in other discussions of those leaders throughout that dictionary.

Wisdom literature tells us to "shun evil" (Job 28:28; Prov 3:7; 14:16); how do we determine whether another individual's or church's behavior warrants our disdain?

I am placing our own divisiveness in the spotlight because I think our tendency to define ourselves by our differences has spiraled unhelpfully. There are jokes told about the ever-finer splits within certain denominations, along the lines of "you follow the 1792 declaration rather than the 1799—heretic scum!" that hit far too close to the truth. To me, the history of Protestantism and evangelicalism has been shaped substantially by separation from certain mainstream views or other majorities. We have come to define ourselves as much by what we stand against as what we stand for. I think this has been especially the case where Christianity has been ascendant; "everyone" is a believer, so my own identity stems from that which marks me as different. I suspect our denominational heritages bequeath us a theological mindset that tolerates or even favors dissent. I think the Western world also foments a cultural mind-set whereby I delineate myself and my tribe in contradistinction to others. We can readily spot the teenage rebel who (following an ironically conformist trend) seeks to stand out from the crowd. Especially if modern advertising is to be believed, the rest of us are equally keen to be lauded as different, just without the tattoos or the excessive eyeliner.

Does Scripture actually encourage us to embrace and emphasize difference? In my own musings, I am not especially convinced that there is much warrant for

distinctions among believers. Of course I am not refer-
ring to our taste in fashion or cars or mobile operating
systems. Yet the Bible contains many more calls to unity
than I expected. It does not seem to exemplify as much
diversity as I might have supposed.

Certainly there are examples where the boundaries
in view concern significant, black-and-white, "first-
order" issues. Some of the confrontations in Acts are
concerned with what is required for salvation (e.g.,
Acts 15:1, 11). A showdown between Paul and Peter is not
just about personal dining preferences but, again, concerns "the truth of the gospel" (Gal 2:5, 14). The problem
that faces most of us is trying to determine whether
our church's stance on baptism or alcohol or environ-
mentalism or abortion is a first-order "gospel" issue.
Indeed, the particular problem extends beyond just
what we abstractly think and believe to how these
truths are expressed in our behavior toward one another. A concomitant problem is that those of us who
are more focused on tasks than on people and relationships can wrongly presume that the end disregards the
means. Peter brought the gospel to Cornelius and his
household but was lambasted particularly for eating
with these Gentiles (Acts 11:3). Similarly, when Peter
and Barnabas ceased to dine with Gentiles at Antioch,
Paul's concern was not that anyone uttered a dubious
christology or that the Gentiles were deprived of food
(Gal 2:11–14). We hear—repeatedly—that a correct
belief that leads people to call Jesus "Lord" does not

automatically translate into saving action (e.g., Matt 25:41–46; Luke 6:46–49; Jas 2:14–18).[12]

It is worth noting that some communities have sought scriptural warrant for their segregationism. One denomination puts great stock in Romans 16:17, where Paul warns against "those who cause dissensions and obstacles contrary to the doctrine you have learned. Avoid them" (HCSB). The interpretation suggests that Paul is warning against any divisiveness—even that caused by other believers—and sanctions divisions between and within denominations. The irony of the cause and effect makes this interpretation difficult.[13] Put to similar ends, though sounding quite converse, 1 Corinthians 11:19 can be read as Paul's pragmatic shrug as he resignedly accepts that "there have to be factions among you." Most commentators, however, find both verses not to endorse quibbling over second-order issues but to reinforce separation only over primary matters of salvation. Protection from external threats is encouraged; internal divisions are a sign of immaturity. We do not find here any escape clauses that permit or expect wildly differing views among believers.[14]

---

12. Cf. Fred B. Craddock, "Christian Unity and the New Testament: A Conversation between Luke and John," *Mid-Stream* 27 (1988): 4–8. "Christians can believe right and behave wrong" (7).

13. See the historical survey and (unconvincing) exegetical exploration of William J. Hassold, " 'Avoid Them': Another Look at Romans 16:17–20," *Currents in Theology and Mission* 27 (2000): 196–208.

14. On 1 Cor 11:19 see the helpful proposal of R. Alastair Campbell, "Does Paul Acquiesce in Divisions at the Lord's Supper?" *Novum Testamentum* 33 (1991): 61–70, that Paul's words are *decrying* these divisions.

Yet, *within a relatively forceful expectation of unity* there is some recognition of diversity. We have already noted the prominence of the "body" metaphor and the way it is regularly invoked in calls for unity. So it is significant that the same metaphor recognizes, tolerates, and promotes diversity within overarching unity. Indeed, we find the apostolic leaders themselves alternating between Semitic and Hellenistic names and adjusting their choice of cultural identity and language as needed. Neither do we have a monochrome presentation of the life of Jesus, but four separate Gospels pitched at different readers and their needs. Some of our pastoral and scholarly energies are expended on holding together apparently disparate views—think Paul "versus" James on the place of deeds.[15] We might overlook how frequently diversity is recognized and practiced. Even the persistent calls to unity concede that the church is not there yet.

FIRST STEPS FORWARD

How then should we balance this recognition of diversity amid an overriding momentum toward unity? It is important to note that, in many conflicts, there may indeed be a more correct stance to promote. In Romans, Paul overtly aligns himself with the "strong" even as he calls for peace and mutual edification of those who are "weak" (e.g., Rom 14:13–21). He has earlier indicated the benefits that Jews enjoy over Gentiles (Rom 3:1–2; 9:4–5),

---

15. Several of these points are made by Larry W. Hurtado, "You've Got to 'Accentuate the Positive': Thinking about Differences Biblically," *Scottish Bulletin of Evangelical Theology* 30 (2012): 21–29.

describing them as botantically authentic in contrast with later engraftments (Rom 11:13-24). In Antioch, Paul is confident that his approach to table fellowship is more "in line with the truth of the gospel" than that of Peter and Barnabas (Gal 2:11-14 NIV). And Acts is at pains to spell out how Paul, Peter, Barnabas, and others stand together against a more Pharisaical view of Christian salvation (Acts 15 and beyond).[16] On other occasions, diversity is accepted if not perhaps encouraged.

Telling the difference is, of course, the challenge before us. And this volume is one attempt to guide the church in discerning when a behavior is of utmost importance and crucial to gospel orthodoxy, and when it might be a secondary and tolerable alternative. Many of us have a sense of how to navigate any differences once we have identified them, and we protest that the sole problem lies in the initial identification of which differences are acceptable and which are worth fighting over. Certainly if there were simple litmus tests available, many disputes might be more easily constrained and resolved.

I wonder whether the very solutions to differences might contribute to our identification and classification of them. If we consider more the process and purpose involved, we may better learn when to pursue them.

---

16. For a strong insistence that the debate at Jerusalem forms the central turning point of the entire Acts narrative, see Brian S. Rosner, "The Progress of the Word," in *Witness to the Gospel: The Theology of Acts*, ed. I. Howard Marshall and David G. Peterson (Grand Rapids: Eerdmans, 1998), 215-33, esp. 227.

I think there are four initial steps that move us in the right direction.

Weighty Matters

I think it is helpful to appreciate that the kinds of issues that come up for debate are indeed matters that have the potential to appear worth fighting over. Although some quarters of the church still dispute matters of music or fashion, it seems to me that many of us can identify those as secondary matters. That said, where a believer thinks that such issues do move us closer to or further away from God, the matter has accrued sufficient weight to be treated thoughtfully. So we are dealing with issues that present themselves as matters of salvation and Christian identity. Our challenge is to gauge to what extent this is true, so that we can then respond appropriately.

Related to this is the invisible and integrated nature of culture. It can be hard to untangle how much our preference for a certain Bible translation or a particular liturgical tradition really is linked with matters of correct doctrine and how much it is a part of our cultural identity. Cross-cultural missionaries struggle with such boundaries daily. Of course the solution is not a rampant relativism. While Western culture readily pushes us each to our own truth and our own preferences, the church cannot continue to splinter into as many flavors as there are believers.

So we must be prepared to embark on potentially heated discussions, where the stakes appear to one or both sides as carrying substantial weight. Too easily we might dismiss an interlocutor and fail to appreciate the importance of an issue *in their eyes*. The examples in my colleagues' contributions each demonstrate ways in which this might be better achieved or squandered. On no occasion are we called to settle for disharmony. There are occasions where we might resolve to tolerate secondary preferences. But there are clear instructions and examples against carving out our superior niche and pronouncing every alternative as false. Although God's warning to Peter carried a specific cultic sense, I suspect there are multiple contexts in which he might chastise us: "Do not call anything impure that God has made clean" (Acts 10:15 NIV).

A Simple Test

The weight of a dispute can be simply tested by whether we think a particular stance qualifies or disqualifies someone as a believer. Although only a rough guide, it seems to me that issues of "primary" importance— concerning which there must be unity—tend to be more vertical and concern our relationship with God. Secondary matters, where there may be diversity, tend to revolve more around our horizontal relationships, with other believers.

This generalization may help explain potential confusion, not least when one kind of action seems to bear different weight at different places in Scripture. In Acts 15 (and some of his letters) Paul fights strenuously against circumcision as a step toward salvation. Yet the instant Paul determines to proclaim this decision more widely, he circumcises Timothy to minimize offense to Jews (Acts 16:1-3).[17] Likewise, Paul can readily insist that various dietary observances carry no salvific consequences (e.g., Rom 14:17, 20; 1 Cor 8:8; 10:25-27), yet he will readily acquiesce when they might harm his horizontal relationships (e.g., Rom 14:19-21; 1 Cor 8:9-13; 10:28). Conversely, Paul boasts in his willingness to eat kosher food when it aids harmony (1 Cor 9:20; compare Acts 21:17-26) yet condemns Peter and Barnabas when the same restrictions impinge on salvation (Gal 2:11-14).

Of course, gauging whether a matter is of primary, salvific importance can be difficult to determine, especially if the heat of dispute clouds our objectivity. Neither should leniency in certain areas—some that we might feel to border on matters of salvation—be mistaken for surrender on all issues. We must rightly preserve some matters as being of the first order without making *all* matters primary. Yet we must deem many issues to be secondary, without unconditionally surrendering everything. It can be all too easy to peremptorily measure the theological temperature of another individual or group by sampling their views of passages like Genesis 1 or 1 Timothy 2 or Revelation 20. Even more difficult are those occasions or issues where a "horizontal" difference is perceived or expressed as being of "vertical" consequence. The Pauline examples above illustrate exactly that.

---

17. The contrast is even more stark if, with a growing number of commentators, we treat Acts 16:1-5 as a continuation of Paul's *first* missionary journey.

A Slow Response

The corollary of the second step is that we ought to be cautious of simplistic, knee-jerk reactions. It is very easy to produce our favorite shibboleths, to reduce complex theological mazes to an easy black-or-white kind of test. Lindsay Wilson reviews for us the events of Joshua 22, where a response that is hasty *and apparently theologically sound* threatens to bring civil war to the twelve tribes of Israel.

A moment's thought yields several biblical examples, especially the ones raised just above. Each is concerned with important, theologically weighty matters. And a particular stance might be defended from a hasty invoking of a narrow selection of scriptures. But wider investigation reminds us that these examples are "context sensitive." We are right to insist that believers *need* not be circumcised—but we cannot deny that Paul *encourages* circumcision on occasions. He even answers his own rhetorical question in a way that might surprise us: "What advantage, then, is there in being a Jew, or what value is there in circumcision? Much in every way!" (Rom 3:1-2 NIV). Indeed, embarrassing though it may be to some of us who revere Paul as the apostle to the Gentiles, he is not averse to apparently purposeless Jewish behavior (e.g., Acts 18:18; 21:17-26; 1 Cor 9:20). This from the same man who complains to the Galatians that "you are observing special days, and months, and seasons, and years. I am afraid that my work for you may have been wasted" (Gal 4:10-11 NRSV)! And we are right to enjoy the delights of a full menu, although we find a number of Old Testament and New Testament passages that, taken in isolation, appear to demand restrictions.

I wonder whether religious arrogance or extremism stems from an overconfidence on issues that are not as cut and dried as we might like them to be. Topics where the testimony of Scripture is fluid across time or cultures are particularly challenging. I would hazard a guess and suggest that believers with a more rigid approach to Christian behavior may be less sympathetic to (or less familiar with or less practiced at) changes that occur over time and between Testaments. Some traditions treat Scripture as a synchronic monolith, ignoring or denying what others see as diachronic progression.

Put simply, I wonder whether we have *cultural* tendencies to seek hard-and-fast rules, to mark out our territory or to lay down our authority. We can find many examples where the hasty application of an isolated proof text is at odds with other equally authoritative passages of Scripture. For a generation increasingly accustomed to instant answers from Google and Wikipedia, we may need to slow our pace of response.

A Repeated Solution

As we recognize real issues with real believers involved, as we ponder the test of primacy and salvation, as we restrain ourselves from hasty and simplistic responses, we do well to appreciate a fourth step. The New Testament offers a repeated solution to disputable matters: humility.

The word is readily recognized by Christians. We might be surprised to learn that it was effectively a swearword to the Gentiles to whom Paul commonly wrote; Greek readers likely despised the apostle's calls to weakness.[18] For all our familiarity with the word, in my opinion too many evangelicals are disinterested in theological generosity toward those who differ from some norm.

Yet the call away from hasty judgment is far more prevalent than we might wish, and it is readily found to be a theme of New Testament contributors beyond Paul. We have already seen Jesus' prayer in John 17 for unity among believers. He has already given his disciples "a new command: Love one another" (John 13:34–35 HCSB). The example he invokes is himself. And the example he has just furnished has been his servile washing of their feet, which Peter, for one, resisted. Shortly Jesus will repeat himself in further detail (John 15:12–17). Similarly, we regularly memorize Mark 10:45, especially because of Jesus' overt awareness of his self-sacrificial "ransom." We must not overlook the first purpose Jesus gives in that verse ("not to be served but to serve") and that this verse is itself an explanation ("For ...") for Jesus' rebuke; his power-hungry disciples should be aiming to be "servant" among their peers and "slave of all"!

The same is found in Philippians 2. Again, the hymn to Jesus is popular for its christological contributions. But it is itself an extended illustration of the humility

---

18. E.g., G. Walter Hansen, *The Letter to the Philippians*, Pillar New Testament Commentaries (Grand Rapids: Eerdmans, 2009), 114–16; Ben Witherington III, *The Letters to Philemon, the Colossians, and the Ephesians* (Grand Rapids: Eerdmans, 2007), 284.

to which Paul calls his congregation. And we do well to note how humility itself is one of the basic ingredients for restoring unity in Philippi. Let us follow Paul's logic:

> Therefore,
>> if there is encouragement in Christ,
>> if any consolation of love,
>> if any fellowship of the Spirit,
>> if any compassion and sympathy,
> complete my joy:
>> think the same,
>> having the same love,
>> being co-souled,
>> thinking the one thing ... (Phil 2:1–2).

Paul's instructions are indeed this terse in other translations: "Be of the same mind, having the same love, being in full accord and of one mind" (NRSV). The call to unity could hardly be phrased more forcefully.

As if Paul's directive were not strong enough, he proceeds to explain further how such unity can be achieved:

> ... not according to self-ambition nor according to empty conceit
>> but with humility regarding one another as surpassing yourselves;
> not each looking to your own interests
>> but everyone to the interests of others.

It is here that Paul invokes the famous call to share the same attitude as Christ Jesus, who gave away his own rights and privileges and *humbled* himself, even to human death on a cross. There are other Pauline examples to explore, either below or elsewhere (e.g., 2 Tim 2:25; Rom 12:16, 18).

The same points are made also by Peter in a text we have already considered. As he comes to summarize several chapters of his teaching, he reiterates almost exactly what we have heard from Paul:

> To sum up, all of you must be
>   same-minded,
>   sympathetic,
>   brother-loving,
>   compassionate,
>   humble-minded ...
> for to this you were called (1 Pet 3:8–9).

I have laid out the passage in the chiastic structure that several scholars entertain.[19] If the concentric pairs are intentional, then Peter ties together thinking the *same* and thinking *humbly*. The next pair suggests that Christians should strive toward being united in their feelings as well, with the central goal of this unified thinking and feeling being the ability to express love for other believers. Sounds a lot like Jesus' instructions to Peter and his peers in John's Gospel.

Again, the ancient world was prone to *avoid* such humility. This may explain the prominence of the potentially distasteful instruction among New Testament

---

19. Peter H. Davids, *The First Epistle of Peter*, New International Commentary on the New Testament (Grand Rapids: Eerdmans, 1990), 124–25; Thomas R. Schreiner, *1, 2 Peter, Jude*, New American Commentary 37 (Nashville: Broadman & Holman, 2003), 163–64; Greg W. Forbes, *1 Peter*, Exegetical Guide to the Greek New Testament (Nashville: B&H Academic, 2014), 108.

authors. Its repetition may elicit our own discomfort with the term, found continually at the core of so many application sections. Indeed, as Rosner shows for Romans 14, being right is not actually as important as being humble, as tolerating suboptimal theology and practice for the sake of others.

CONCLUSION

Disputable matters are confronting us. And our survey here suggests each disputable matter is not just a single challenge but one that conjures several others. We are called to navigate such disputes for an overarching unity in our thinking. We need to do this despite the recognition of diversity that exists within the body of Christ. And we are expected to admit that pastoral humility will sometimes prioritize gentle tolerance of diversity over rigid theological exactness. We are instructed, in no uncertain terms, to avoid the natural competitiveness and self-justification toward which all humans gravitate.

A final example reiterates each of the points highlighted. They coalesce in several Bible passages but perhaps nowhere more clearly than in Ephesians 4. The final line recorded from 1 Peter 3 (the passage we have just left) is not insignificant: "for to this you were called." Paul likewise regularly bases his ethical injunctions on Christian identity. We might summarize his frequent call as "Be what you are." Indeed, we find this as Paul turns from theory to application in Ephesians. He has spent three chapters praising God for intertwining Jews and Gentiles into one new temple, creating for himself "one new humanity ... thus making peace"

(Eph 2:15 NRSV). The apostle now turns to the practical outworkings of this theological reality. As with Peter, Paul calls the Ephesians to live up to the calling they have already received: "Therefore, I urge you … to walk worthily of the calling to which you were called" (Eph 4:1).

Paul proceeds to explain, in some detail, that this "calling" of believers involves a whole lot of unity. Next, Paul explains the means for achieving this. A worthy walk is accomplished:

> with all humility and gentleness,
> with long-suffering,
> being tolerant of one another in love,
> being eager/diligent to keep the unity of the Spirit
>   in the bond of peace.

As if this language of "unity" and "peace" (achieved by "humility" and other attitudes) were not enough, Paul then launches into his famous refrain:

> One body and one Spirit,
> just as you also were called in one hope of
>   your calling,
> one Lord, one faith, one baptism, one God and
>   Father of all …

Paul's call to unity and its theological collection of "ones" not only introduce the next few lines but, indeed, give shape to all the remaining instructions that comprise the latter half of this letter.[20]

The call to unity is certainly played out in the next paragraphs of Ephesians 4. Here Paul introduces one of his famous lists of gifts in the Christian community. Again, we find recognition of the differences that exist among believers; there is no expectation of cloned unicity. Yet these varied gifts are given for the sake of unity, for "equipping" the saints—that same surgical idea of "restoring" or "reunifying" or "resetting" (1 Cor 1:10). Paul's goal is the edification of Christ's body, the same metaphor that recognizes diverse elements within a single whole, an image that Paul pursues for several verses. Indeed, his overarching goal is that this body achieves maturity, which Paul describes as reaching "unity in the faith and in the knowledge of the Son of God" (Eph 4:13 NIV).

Thus we find yet another express call for believers to work hard and diligently toward unity. Paul recognizes the diversity that exists in the body of Christ, whether those are natural distinctions to celebrate or unwanted fractures that need to be mended. And right in the middle of his calls for unity and corporate maturity, Paul furnishes a string of tools to achieve this, a list starting with humility. For those of us uncomfortable enough to try to dilute such calls to unity, we must remember the substantial overlap between various instructions from

---

20. Peter T. O'Brien, *The Letter to the Ephesians*, Pillar New Testament Commentary (Grand Rapids: Eerdmans, 1999), 272–73; Klyne R. Snodgrass, *Ephesians*, New International Version Application Commentary (Grand Rapids: Zondervan, 1996), 194.

Paul, and even between Paul and Peter. What we find in Ephesians 4 is echoed in other passages like Philippians 2, Colossians 3, Romans 12, and 1 Peter 3.[21]

Believers are clearly called to maintain the unity bestowed by the Spirit. We already enjoy something of it—though it also appears possible to squander this gift. As we probe the boundaries of whether we may differ, the Bible calls for a substantial focus on avoiding divisions, resetting broken bonds, and striving for wholeness and maturity in the body of Christ. "Walk worthily of the calling to which you were called ... being eager and diligent to keep the unity of the Spirit in the bond of peace."

21. Cf. O'Brien, *Ephesians*, 277; Michaels, *1 Peter*, 174–75.

CHAPTER 2

UNITY MATTERS

A Study of Joshua 22:1-34

Lindsay Wilson

INTRODUCTION

Why should we look at Joshua 22 if we are trying to explore how to deal with disputable matters in today's complex world? As an Old Testament specialist, I am used to questions like this, based on the assumption that the Old Testament is of little value for Christians today. But in fact, Paul wrote that "all scripture [mostly what we now call the Old Testament] is inspired by God and useful for teaching, reproof, correction and training in righteousness" (2 Tim 3:16). On the assumption that Paul is right (and the practice of many Christians is wrong), we should look to the Old Testament, as well as the New Testament, as a rich source of information, principles, and goals.

The issues of Joshua 22 are disputable matters, for the following reasons:

1. Matters of religious practice can often be sources of dispute between believers.[1]

2. The action of building the altar was ambiguous until it was explained—like many religious practices, building programs, and other new initiatives.[2]

3. Building this altar (within the limits of 22:5) was a matter of freedom. The people were not commanded to build it, but they were also not prohibited from building it. This was not a right/wrong issue.

4. The lack of communication created a misunderstanding. One group built the altar for a particular (legitimate) purpose, but another group interpreted their action as having a different significance.

Even so, out of all the Old Testament, why should we study Joshua 22? At one level, it contains useful principles and lessons about handling differences among God's people. Indeed, the story is distinctive in that it does not simply record a conflict or broken relationship, but it also shows how God's people came to a successful

1. R. M. Billings, *"Israel Served the Lord": The Book of Joshua as Paradoxical Portrait of Faithful Israel* (Notre Dame, IN: University of Notre Dame Press, 2013), 91, suggests, "The story illustrates the negotiation of a cultic dispute between two groups of Israelites without the benefit of a civil leader or a divine word spoken directly to the situation."

2. R. D. Nelson, *Joshua: A Commentary*, Old Testament Library (Louisville: Westminster John Knox, 1997), 246, refers to the "enigmatic act of altar building."

resolution of the issues in dispute. The remoteness of this chapter might then encourage people to look elsewhere in the Bible for other, lesser-known passages where God's people deal with disputable matters.

THE SETTING

The setting of this passage in the book of Joshua is very significant in light of its emphasis on the unity of all Israel. It depicts God's chosen people as united in serving him, going out in battle and conquest as one, with only occasional blips. Although they were twelve tribes, they worked side by side. Even the two-and-a-half tribes on the east bank of the Jordan—who had already possessed their land—crossed over the Jordan to fight with the other tribes. They worked together with their fellow Israelites and were not primarily twelve tribes but one nation. Unity is much easier if groups are working in tandem for a common goal of building up God's kingdom.

Yet all this threatens to fall apart in Joshua 22. The kind of unity modeled in the book of Joshua can only be based on a common commitment to the one true God. In Joshua 22, the nine-and-a-half tribes in the western part of the land believe that the two-and-a-half tribes who returned to the other side of the Jordan have given up the faith and put all of Israel in danger. How did this come about?

JOSHUA'S EXHORTATION (JOSH 22:1-8)

At the beginning of the passage, Joshua bid farewell to the eastern tribes, having commended them as being faithful to God, loyal to their fellow Israelites, and obedient to their leaders (Josh 22:1-3). He permitted them to return to their lands across the river (Josh 22:4).

When he sent them off he instructed them to keep doing what they have already done—being wholeheartedly committed to God. Joshua instructed them in 22:5 about their priorities in their new setting. They must be very careful about continuing to be faithful to God, which he described as observing the command (charge) and law (instruction) as given by Moses (Josh 22:5a).[3] The rest of the verse fleshes out these concepts for those returning to the eastern side of the Jordan:

- Love the Lord your God.

- Walk in obedience to him.

- Keep his commands.

- Hold fast to him.

- Serve him with all your heart and with all your soul (life).

These are not distinct spheres of life but a way of saying "serve with your whole life," with all you have and are.

The issue was never whether they should have crossed back over the Jordan. That was a given. Joshua gave them his blessing (Josh 22:6, 7b), Moses had already

---

3. E. Assis, " 'For It Shall Be a Witness between Us': A Literary Reading of Josh 22," *Scandinavian Journal of the Old Testament* 18 (2004): 210, observes, "Joshua's instruction to the Transjordanian tribes to keep God's commandments in v 5 foreshadows the second part of the story, which depicts the concern that they have not followed this instruction."

given them the land (e.g., Josh 22:7a), and Joshua sent them back to the eastern side with the spoils of victory (Josh 22:7b–8). They would have been disobedient to stay rather than return. The issue was always how they were to live and continue serving God once they had crossed back over the Jordan.

UNITY QUICKLY DESTROYED
(JOSH 22:9-12)

As they went on their way, the eastern tribes were still one with the rest of Israel. Verse 9 (see also Josh 22:4) reinforces the rightness of their return to the other side of the Jordan, describing their holdings to the east of the Jordan as the land acquired "by the command of the Lord through Moses." This permission had already been recorded in Joshua 1:12–18, where Joshua insisted that Reuben, Gad, and half of Manasseh send their fighters over into Canaan to assist in the conquest of the rest of the land, and only then (*but then!*) to settle down on the eastern side.

What changed the status quo? The trigger was a building program—the building of an altar altered everything. Verses 10–11 suggest that the altar was constructed in the land of Canaan.[4] It was *an imposing altar*

---

4. There is some scholarly dispute about whether the altar was located on the eastern or western side of the Jordan. L. D. Hawk, *Every Promise Fulfilled: Contesting Plots in Joshua* (Louisville: Westminster John Knox, 1991), 122, argues that the narrator's description in v. 10a implies it was located on the western bank of the Jordan, while v. 11b suggests that the westerners locate it on the east bank. R. Boling, *Joshua*, Anchor Bible (Garden City, NY: Doubleday, 1982), 512, suggests: "The reference could be to any

and therefore clearly visible to the east-bankers in their homeland.[5] Building an altar is, like many unexplained actions, ambiguous by itself. It is hard to discern the builders' intent; it is easy to think the worst, to misread and be suspicious of the builders' actions; and there is a deafening silence about the function of this big altar.[6] We are not told at first why the eastern tribes built the altar, nor are we told in Joshua 22:12 why the other tribes thought it was wrong. Yet the vehemence of their reaction suggests that they thought the groups in Canaan were seeking to establish a cultic site to rival Shiloh. R. M. Billings seems to accurately describe the perception of the western tribes: "If the altar in

---

point in the Jordan Valley, on either side of the river. Each succeeding phrase, ostensibly written to further pinpoint the area, only sustains the obscurity of the location." J. G. McConville and S. N. Williams, *Joshua*, Two Horizons Old Testament Commentary (Grand Rapids: Eerdmans, 2010), 84, argue that where the altar was in relation to the Jordan is "tantalizingly difficult to determine." However, N. H. Snaith, "The Altar at Gilgal: Joshua xxii 23-29," *Vetus Testamentum* 28 (1978): 330–35, outlines sensible reasons for the altar being located on the eastern side of the Jordan, and this view is adopted in modern translations such as the NRSV, ESV, and NIV.

5. The altar is literally described in v. 10 as "big to seeing." Robert L. Hubbard, *Joshua*, New International Version Application Commentary (Grand Rapids: Zondervan, 2009), 485, colorfully paraphrases this as "so big you couldn't miss it."

6. Nelson, *Joshua*, 253, observes that crucial information is delayed until vv. 27–28 to increase suspense in the story. Billings, *Israel Served the Lord*, 83–84, suggests that the withholding of this explicit information draws the reader into the dispute, although they would have known of the easterners' former faithfulness in vv. 1–5. It is commonly the case in conflicts that the facts are not clearly known by both sides.

fact turns out to be an expression of rebellion against YHWH, it threatens to destroy the unity of the newly settled people of YHWH, instigating division and strife within just as rest from external forces at last has become possible."[7] What is clear among all the confusion is that the westerners took this matter so seriously that they gathered for war (Josh 22:12).

A DELEGATION CONFRONTS THE EASTERN TRIBES (JOSH 22:13–19)

As the story unfolds, it becomes evident that both sides had a strong commitment to being faithful to Yahweh, but the westerners interpreted the building of this altar differently. The two-and-a-half tribes on the east side were trying to shore up that faithfulness in future generations, but to the nine-and-a-half tribes on the west, it looked like the easterners were compromising an essential aspect of loyalty to God. Since the westerners believed that God's honor was at stake, they were prepared to take a costly stand and initiate warfare.

Before doing so they appointed some key people to check out the facts (Josh 22:13–14). Since the matter concerned proper worship, they chose a priest, Phinehas, to represent them. Phinehas had already risen to prominence for his zeal in dealing with the Israelite idolaters at Baal-Peor (Num 25:1–9).[8] If he speared an adulterous

---

7. Billings, *Israel Served the Lord*, 80.

8. B. Organ, "Pursuing Phinehas: A Synchronic Reading," *Catholic Biblical Quarterly* 63 (2001): 209, describes him as "the faithful priest who can be counted on to defend the proper worship of YHWH."

couple then, what might he do now when given authority by "all Israel"?

Since the matter also concerned the unity of Israel,
a representative of each of the ten remaining tribes
went along, presumably so none would be disenfran-
chised. These ten men were leaders of the community
(described as such in 22:30; head of family divisions
among clans in 22:14), whose voices would carry weight
to influence the rest when they returned. We should
note that they did not appoint a few token, low-level
people just so they could say that they checked on the
facts. The task of reconciliation based on truth was too
important for that. The tribes sent men who were "the
highest level of leadership in Israel, the Israelite equivalent of a presidential cabinet."[9] Thus they were prepared to devote valuable resources to the process.

The concern about the building of an altar seems
grounded in Moses' teaching in Deuteronomy 12, which
states that the Israelites were only to offer sacrifices at
the place that God would choose. While that would one
day be Jerusalem, it was currently in Shiloh, where the
ark was located. This directive was designed to ensure
purity of worship once the people entered the land.
Breaching it would lead to both unfaithfulness to God
and the destruction of Israel's unity.

Those in the west saw the altar building as breaking faith with the God of Israel (Josh 22:16), rebelling
against God (Josh 22:16), and turning away from him
(Josh 22:18). Since they thought this action similar to the

---

9. Hubbard, *Joshua*, 487. There is no explanation why Joshua himself was not involved in the delegation.

sin of Baal of Peor (Josh 22:17; see Num 25), or the sin of Achan (Josh 22:20), they believed it would have an effect on all Israel, not just those who sinned (Josh 22:18b).[10] Their underlying view appears to be that whenever other tribes permitted sin, they could expect God's judgment on those who did not stand against it. If only God's people today would take such an admirable stance, correcting error and speaking out for truth!

Does this mean that diversity among God's people is a problem? It largely depends on what kind of diversity is at issue. Of course, some diversity is delightful (e.g., race, age, gender, social and financial status), but diverse views over central truths are an entirely different matter. In New Testament terms, since the church lives under the kingship of Christ, church discipline is central (e.g., Matt 18:15–20).

The westerners propose a solution in Joshua 22:19. They were willing to think laterally and sacrificially.

---

10. A. G. Auld, "Re-telling the Disputed 'Altar' in Joshua 22," in *The Book of Joshua*, ed. E. Noort, Bibliotheca Ephemeridum Theologicarum Lovaniensium 250 (Leuven: Peeters, 2012), 285–86, raises the possibility that the two groups may be motivated by different traditions and scriptures. Certainly this is often the case in conflicts over disputable matters. He argues that the westerners are viewing what has happened through the lens of the worship of Baal of Peor in Num 25 as well as Num 16, where the sin of one man affected the others. The easterners respond with echoes of Pss 50 and 44, as well as a reference to Genesis by claiming a parallel with Jacob, who was pursued by the stronger Laban. He concludes that "The westerners invoke the book of Numbers, and the easterners reply by recalling Psalms and Genesis." If this is the case, it is a salutary reminder of the danger of only looking at those biblical texts that support one's position on a disputable matter.

They propose that the tribes east of the Jordan could take a share in their land west of the Jordan. They seemed to have thought that the easterners built the altar to cleanse the land, which had been defiled in some way, perhaps by pagan worship. This showed a generosity of spirit—they were willing to share their land with their fellow Israelites. The offer was enormously costly. Those on the eastern side of the Jordan were, in rough terms, about a quarter of the population of those in Canaan (two-and-a-half tribes in the east; nine-and-a-half tribes in the west). That would be a massive influx, a bit like a nation such as Australia choosing to accept and incorporate 5–6 million refugees at one time.[11]

A CONCERN FOR UNITY AND BELONGING, NOT REBELLION (JOSH 22:20-29)

What did the accused tribes say? They started with a description of who God is (Josh 22:22 NIV): "The Mighty One, God, the LORD!" It is clear that they had no intention to worship any other deity at this altar.

Then they agreed with the principle that, if they had rebelled against God, they deserved to be put to death (Josh 22:22b). Verse 23 fills out this concept by making the issue more specific: May God punish us if we have built this altar to turn away from God, which would have been demonstrated by them using the altar to offer sacrifices. The eastern tribes did not get defensive

---

11. D. Jobling, *The Sense of Biblical Narrative. Structural Analyses in the Hebrew Bible II*, Journal for the Study of the Old Testament Supplement Series (Sheffield, UK: Sheffield Academic, 1986), 99, interestingly calls the story "a narrative of gross implausibility."

or abusive; they defused the situation by building common ground and clarifying the factual issue. The real issue was the nature of this altar and its intended use.

Their explanation continues in 22:24–29. They outlined the kind of scenario that led them to build the altar. It was based on an understandable fear (Josh 22:24): They wanted to ensure that they would not be kicked out of the community who feared the Lord (Josh 22:25). The Jordan was a big natural barrier.[12] They were outside the land in one sense; and we later see tribal disintegration and rivalry in the period of the book of Judges, which followed Joshua. Several hints in the descriptions in the chapter give some grounds for the fears of the eastern tribes. In Joshua 22:11, 12, 13, the nine-and-a-half tribes are described as the Israelites, implying the others are not. The contrast of 22:11 is between "the Israelites" (those west of the Jordan) and the Reubenites, Gadites, and half-tribe of Manasseh (those east of the Jordan). The passage speaks about the eastern tribes as if they were not, in some sense, among the true Israelites. Then 22:12 says "when the people of Israel heard of it, the whole assembly of the Israelites [the nine-and-a-half tribes] gathered at Shiloh." Were the easterners part of Israel or not? Verse 13 starts with "the Israelites," again meaning those in the nine-and-a-half tribes.

The eastern tribes had built the altar so that they would continue to be regarded as genuine members of

---

12. Hawk, *Every Promise Fulfilled*, 121, notes that "The Jordan is viewed as a boundary which effectively separates the eastern tribes from their kinspeople in the promised land, thus negating a sense of unity."

the people of God (Josh 22:25b). They say a similar thing in 22:27b, showing a desire to avoid a future situation in which the majority nine-and-a-half tribes told the westerners' descendants, "You have no share in the Lord." In relation to the specific issue of 22:23—whether the altar is to be a place of rival sacrifice—they twice say that the altar was not for burnt offerings or sacrifices (Josh 22:26, 28). In addition, they clarify the matter in the summary (Josh 22:29 NIV): "Far be it from us to rebel against the LORD and turn away from him today by building an altar for burnt offerings, grain offerings and sacrifices, other than the altar of the LORD our God that stands before his tabernacle."

The westerners had given no explicit explanation, however, to the rest of Israel. Perhaps those living on the eastern side thought that the size of the altar and its location on the west bank made it obvious that it served no sacrificial purpose. David Howard makes the telling point that:

> The altar's location should have been a clue from the beginning as to its purpose. Significantly, the Transjordan tribes did not build it on their side of the Jordan, but across the river from where they would live. It served little useful purpose to them there; for it to have been used regularly to offer sacrifices, it would need to have been east of the river.[13]

---

13. David M. Howard, *Joshua*, New American Commentary (Nashville: Broadman & Holman, 1998), 414. E. Assis, "The Position and Function of Jos 22 in the Book of Joshua," *Zeitschrift für die alttestamentliche Wissenschaft* 116 (2004): 538, also argues

Maybe it never occurred to them that, after proving their loyalty to the other tribes in battle, anyone would suspect them of giving up the true faith.[14] L. D. Hawk, however, views the easterners' response with suspicion. He argues that "the entire explanation seems contrived and the denials are suspiciously passionate," adding that "what is the purpose of an altar, if not to provide a place for sacrifice?"[15] This seems to be reading against the grain of the passage. His suggestion that Phinehas and other leaders are seeking to smooth the matter over does not reflect Phinehas' true character as seen in Numbers 25 and 31.

The western tribes further clarify their motivation, since they do more that simply deny the accusation made. The easterners also outline the positive role this altar was meant to have had. It was a witness between the present and future generations (Josh 22:27–28) that they were committed to worship the true Lord in the right place (Josh 22:27). As the two sides talk, they establish a reasonable amount of common ground: that the Jordan is a barrier, that noncentral sacrifice is wrong, and that the tabernacle is the right place for worship.[16] The westerners built an altar intended to re-mind all Israel of its identity and its unity in worship.

---

that the unusually large dimensions of the altar make it clear that it was not intended for sacrificial use.

14. So Hubbard, *Joshua*, 502.

15. Hawk, *Every Promise Fulfilled*, 127. E. Assis, "Literary Reading," 233, takes a different view and describes the easterners' explanation of their actions as "intelligent and detailed."

16. So Nelson, *Joshua*, 249.

Butler concludes that "the Jordan is a symbol of separation. The altar is a symbol of unity."[17]

THE EXPLANATION ACCEPTED, AND FELLOWSHIP RESTORED (JOSH 22:30-34)

In verse 30 we can see one of the keys to the resolution of this theological conflict, and it is not rocket science. The leaders of one side heard what the other side had to say. That is, they listened to their explanation, trying to understand why they acted as they did. And when they understood, they did not get defensive ("well, it didn't look like that to us") but were pleased. Furthermore, they showed graciousness by acknowledging that God was part of this resolution process ("today we know that the Lord is with us," Josh 22:31a NIV). The representatives of the western tribes accepted the explanation that was given and concluded that the easterners had not been unfaithful. They then reported back to the rest of Israel (Josh 22:32-33), and the passage concludes in 22:34 by setting out that their unity was grounded in a common belief that the Lord is God.

SUMMARY

Looking back over the whole incident, we see an emphasis on the theme of Yahweh's faithfulness (Josh 22:5,

---

17. T. C. Butler, *Joshua*, Word Biblical Commentary (Waco, TX: Word, 1983), 249. Nelson, *Joshua*, 249, agrees that "the altar that begins as the center of the conflict turns out to be an instrument of reconciliation." Hubbard, *Joshua*, 481, also comments that "The problematic action proves to be not apostasy but a witness to loyalty to Yahweh and to his worship at the tabernacle."

16, 18, 19, 25, 29, 31) and the expectation for God's people to respond with faithfulness to his unwavering faithfulness. The key assumption of the passage is that we must have a passion to be faithful to Yahweh. There is no real unity, or settling of differences, without that.

Not every biblical story teaches a lesson. The large amount of unnecessary detail in this chapter suggests the author was drawing attention to the process. J. D. Currid writes, "The story is a good example of conflict resolution in the church."[18] If this process did lead to reconciliation, what did they do right?

Assessing Both Parties

What did the parties do well, and what did they do badly? Let us examine each side in turn. First, the westerners. What did they do badly? We see a number of things emerge from the text. Their first response, for example, was to gather to go to war against the easterners, even before they had made proper inquiries. They acted before they had ascertained the facts. Indeed, they simply assumed that the altar was to be used for sacrifices (Josh 22:16). They obviously carried baggage from the past, afraid that God might do again what he did at Peor (Josh 22:17–18). The explicit reference to Achan (Josh 22:20) reveals that they were at least in part concerned for their own skins, not just for the issue at stake. In their haste, they had forgotten the value of self-examination. Jesus' reminder to take the log of your own

---

18. J. D. Currid, *Strong and Courageous: Joshua Simply Explained*, Welwyn Commentaries (Darlington, UK: EP Books, 2011), 234.

eye before observing the speck in your fellow believer's eye (Matt 7:3–5) is surely relevant here.

Yet, they did some things well. For instance, they were prepared to take action when they thought that major sin was involved. In other words, they cared enough about God's honor, about the people of God, and about the spread of sin, to do something rather than settle for doing nothing. This is commendable. In fairness to them, Y. Adu-Gyamfi notes, "in the Hebrew Bible this is the only instance in which an 'altar' does not function as an altar."[19] In addition, before they attacked, they did send Phinehas and a key leader from each interest group (tribe) affected. Even during the negotiations, they made a generous offer to the easterners to come and share their land (Josh 22:19). They did not come with a closed mind, either: Their representatives accepted at face value the explanation given (Josh 22:30) and reported it back to the others (Josh 22:32), who showed a willingness to be corrected as they accepted the report of their leaders (Josh 22:33).

What about the easterners? Their major fault was that they failed to communicate with the westerners beforehand. A little more forethought could have saved a lot of angst.

Still, they did many things well. When challenged, their first thought was of God (Josh 22:22), and throughout they sought to honor God (Josh 22:27, 29, 34). Their actions appear to have a genuinely godly

---

19. Y. Adu-Gyamfi, "Prevention of Civil War in Joshua 22: Guidelines for African Ethnic Groups," *Old Testament Essays* 26 (2013): 258.

motivation. In addition, they explained their ambiguous action (Josh 22:24–28) when called on to do so. They did not get defensive or abusive but defused the situation by building common ground and clarifying the factual issues. Their goal was honoring God as well. They wanted to preserve the unity of God's people or, perhaps more precisely, they wanted to ensure that their children and subsequent generations would follow the Lord.

Some Ways Forward

By looking at the way in which the two groups reconciled their differences, we may discover some sound principles for resolving differences in theological practice. A recent article by Y. Adu-Gyamfi has argued that the principles in this chapter can be used to prevent civil war among African ethnic groups.[20] I suggest that there are at least four key ways forward here:

1. Do not let differences divide. For example, Robert Hubbard suggests that differences including age and gender, various ethnic or cultural backgrounds, different political views, various denominational backgrounds, and newcomers versus old-timers will lead to each group having a different view of what is a big issue at church, what the church should be doing, and how they should worship.[21] This is a challenge to the Christian church, which is divided by denominations and by independent churches. The solution is not a lowest common denominator—that is, outward, organizational unity. It is rather a unity based on holding core

20. Ibid.
21. Hubbard, *Joshua*, 503–4.

beliefs in common, while being gracious on nonessential, disputable matters.

2. Face up to conflict as an important task. The western tribes, the ones who thought the others had done wrong, did not sweep it under the rug. They thought the easterners intended to worship the Lord according to their own will, not his. They took apostasy so seriously that they put purity above their own lives, not buying peace at any price.

3. Devote your best resources to resolving conflict. The western tribes sent their ablest leaders—the priest Phinehas, who had shown himself zealous for the Lord in the episode at Peor (Num 25:7), and ten chiefs representing all the tribes—to investigate the matter and possibly to restore the offenders, not acting rashly. Jesus commands us to take a witness—even the church's elders—to help sort out a dispute (Matt 18:15-20). To preserve unity among the people of God, this procedure provides for representatives to approach the offending party before the whole community becomes embroiled in a dispute. In Joshua 22, representatives of the people of God successfully resolve the issue.[22]

4. Have a generous spirit. The easterners were willing to sacrifice some of their possessions to restore their brothers—they offered them a spot in their land. Those in the east laid out some common ground, then they explained their actions and their fears. The representatives of those in the west accepted their explanation, and so did the people back home. The problem was

---

22. Adu-Gyamfi, "Prevention of Civil War," 259-60, highlights not only using a delegation but also using people of authority.

solved because they not only confronted but also talked and listened.[23] Indeed, both sides listened graciously. We are called to be clear about gospel issues but generous about matters of style, preference, and freedom.

Joshua 22 makes it clear that unity matters. In this neglected chapter, God's people get back on track. They were different, but they belonged together. They were spread out, but they could be united. They showed themselves faithful to God and generous to each other.

It also illustrates how we can see all the evidence and still draw the wrong conclusion.

---

23. Ibid., 259, reminds us of the importance of trusting others, rather than believing the worst about them without investigation.

CHAPTER 3

WHAT TO DO WHEN CHRISTIANS DIFFER

Disputable Matters in
Romans 14:1–15:7

Brian Rosner

INTRODUCTION

The Apostle Paul is often seen as the gatekeeper of doctrinal purity, and with good reason. His responses to departures from Christian truth are uncompromising:

> As we have said before, so now I repeat, if anyone proclaims to you a gospel contrary to what you received, let that one be accursed (Gal 1:9 NRSV)!

> If someone comes and proclaims another Jesus than the one we proclaimed, or if you receive a different spirit from the one you received, or a different gospel from the one you accepted ... such boasters are false apostles, deceitful workers, disguising themselves as apostles of Christ (2 Cor 11:4, 13 NRSV).

I urge you, brothers and sisters, to keep an eye on those who cause dissensions and offenses, in opposition to the teaching that you have learned; keep away from them. For such people do not serve our Lord Christ, but their own appetites, and by smooth talk and flattery they deceive the hearts of the simple-minded (Rom 16:17–18 NRSV adapted).

Such texts speak for themselves. We are to defend the gospel. Doctrine matters. In view of such texts, differences among Christians over matters of faith and practice might be seen as evidence of a dereliction of duty on the part of Christian leaders to correct those in error, or of ungodly compromise simply for reasons of expedience.

However, these texts tell only one side of the story. Paul also taught that along with matters that are beyond dispute, there are such things as disputable matters, subjects on which Christians may legitimately differ. As it turns out, we owe the language of "disputable matters" to Paul himself. In Romans 14:1 he told the Christians in Rome not to "quarrel over disputable matters" (NIV). Other versions translate the phrase in question as "opinions" (ESV, NRSV), "scruples" (ASV), or "doubtful disputations" (KJV).

Paul's longest and most rigorous teaching on the subject is in Romans 14:1–15:7. The following outline and summary provide an overview of the passage:

1. Mutual Acceptance (Rom 14:1–4)

2. Personal Convictions under Christ's Lordship (Rom 14:5–9)

3. Accountability to God (Rom 14:10–12)

4. Limiting Freedom in Love (Rom 14:13–18)

5. Pursuing Peace and Edification (Rom 14:19–21)

6. Maintaining a Clear Conscience (Rom 14:22–23)

7. The Example of Jesus (Rom 15:1–7)

Paul issues the same instructions at the beginning and end of the unit:

> Accept those whose faith is weak, without quarreling over disputable matters (Rom 14:1).

> Accept one another, just as Christ has accepted you (Rom 15:7).

The verb "accept," *proslambanō*, means "extend a welcome" (compare NRSV).[1] It is used to characterize a positive response to Jesus (Matt 10:40; Luke 8:40; 10:38; John 1:11) and for receiving fellow believers as brothers and sisters in Christ (Acts 15:4; 3 John 10). In practical terms, it can refer to extending hospitality to someone (Acts 28:7). In Luke 15:2 Jesus "*welcomes* outcasts and eats with them."

Paul's call to "accept" or "welcome" other Christians rather than quarreling over disputable matters in Romans 14:1 and 15:7 forms a striking contrast to his advice in Romans 16:17 to "keep away from" or "shun" (*ekklinō*) those who disagree with his teaching.

---

1. W. Bauer, F. W. Danker, W. F. Arndt, and F. W. Gingrich, *A Greek-English Lexicon of the New Testament and Other Early Christian Literature*, 3rd ed. (Chicago: University of Chicago Press, 2000), meaning 4.

In reviewing Paul's teaching in Romans 14–15, we'll consider *how* to behave toward fellow believers when they hold different views on matters of legitimate dispute and *why* we should behave in the way that Paul enjoins. If some things for Paul are of "first importance"—that Christ died for our sins according to Scripture and rose from the dead to give us new life (1 Cor 15:1–7)—others are of a secondary nature. We'll also explore some thoughts on how to distinguish the two at the conclusion of this chapter.

The subject of disputable matters has immense practical importance. You don't have to be a church historian to know of numerous regrettable cases of Christian quarreling needlessly doing terrible harm to churches, not to mention damage to the reputation of God and the gospel. If Paul calls for "peace and mutual upbuilding" (Rom 14:19), we must understand that failing to heed his advice on disputable matters leads to fighting and destructive conflict.

The following investigation of disputable matters in Romans 14–15 can be broken down into four questions:

1. What was in dispute in the Roman churches?

2. How were the two groups behaving?

3. How does Paul want them to behave, and on what grounds does he make his appeal?

4. What was at stake?

CONFLICT IN THE ROMAN CHURCHES

What was in dispute in the Roman churches? In short, they were having a dustup over what to do with certain aspects of the law of Moses. Paul mentions two topics in particular: the restriction of diet (see Rom 14:2, 21) and observing certain days in preference to others (Rom 14:5). John Barclay summarizes the consensus of commentators: "In common with many others, I take these verses to refer to Jewish scruples concerning the consumption of meat considered unclean and the observance of the Sabbath and other Jewish feasts or fasts."[2]

Whereas "the weak" in the church (probably mainly Christians from a Jewish background) kept Jewish kosher laws and observed the Sabbath, "the strong" (mainly Gentile Christians) did not. Paul actually counts himself among the strong (Rom 15:1) and is convinced that the Christian believer may "eat anything" (Rom 14:2). He makes his position clear earlier in Romans when he asserts that believers in Christ are not under the law (Rom 6:14–15; 7:1–6).

Yet, surprisingly, Paul did not insist that all the Christians in Rome agree with him. Peter Adam puts it well:

> If I had been writing Romans 14, I would have told those who were weak in faith, and still kept special days, to sort themselves out, and to know that they are justified by grace through faith, not by keeping special days of Jewish practice. Paul, on the other hand, told the strong in faith to accept

---

2. John   Barclay,   *Pauline   Churches   and   Diaspora   Jews*, Wissenschaftliche Untersuchungen zum Neuen Testament 275 (Tübingen: Mohr Siebeck, 2011), 39. See his full treatment on 37–59 for an illuminating study that arrives at similar conclusions to my own.

the weak in faith, and the weak in faith to accept the strong in faith. Both the strong and the weak are answerable to God, not to each other. So we must allow people to act differently in matters that don't contradict the gospel.[3]

Although Paul is a Jew in terms of his ethnicity and heritage, according to 1 Corinthians 9:20 he apparently no longer understands himself to be a full member of Judaism, and he would not consider himself a Jew if such a person understands their relationship with God to be based on adherence to the Mosaic covenant. In Acts, Luke has Paul call himself a Jew twice (Rom 21:39; 22:3), but significantly, Paul prefers to call himself an "Israelite" in his letters (Rom 9:3–4; 11:1; 2 Cor 11:22; Phil 3:5).

However, Paul was tolerant of Jewish Christians who wished to continue traditional observance. Acts 16:1–3 (where Paul circumcises Timothy) and 21:20–26 (where Paul purifies himself and goes to the temple) are suggestive of Luke's understanding of how Paul would actually behave like a Jew for the sake of the progress of the gospel among Jews. For Paul there is nothing inappropriate about keeping certain laws as a matter of tradition or preference, as long as such law keeping is not imposed on Gentiles, does not become a salvation issue, and does not undermine the fellowship of brothers and sisters in Christ (compare Gal 2:11–14). As he states in 1 Corinthians 9:20, "to the Jews I became like a Jew, to win the Jews. To those under the law I became like one

3. Peter Adam, *Gospel Trials in 1662: To Stay or to Go* (London: Latimer Trust, 2012), 56.

under the law (though I myself am not under the law), so as to win those under the law" (NIV).

On such matters, individuals are to act in accordance with their own convictions (Rom 14:5–6). As Paul states in Romans 14:22, "the faith that you have, keep to yourself before God." In effect, Paul allows for the expression of Jewish cultural tradition, living under the law's direction but not its dominion.[4]

WHAT NOT TO DO WHEN CHRISTIANS DIFFER

How were the weak and the strong behaving toward each other when it came to their differences? The occasional nature of Romans means that the letter does not tell us directly. The Christians in Rome obviously knew, and we may assume that Paul had been informed. In any case, the disputes in Rome were the result of the friction that frequently arose when Paul's law-free gospel was proclaimed to Jews and when Gentile believers were included in the people of God. We can infer a fairly accurate picture from Paul's instructions. What Paul tells them not to do is likely to have been what they were doing or at least tempted to do.

If Paul's admonition to "accept those whose faith is weak" in Romans 14:1 is directed to the strong, the call to "accept one another" in Romans 15:7 is for both groups. We may surmise that by not accepting one another, the weak and the strong believers in Rome were shunning

---

4. See Brian S. Rosner, *Paul and the Law: Keeping the Commandments of God*, New Studies in Biblical Theology 31 (Downers Grove, IL: InterVarsity Press, 2013), chap. 2.

and not extending hospitality to each other (see above on *proslambanō*). However, beyond this general description of the problem, we can discern behaviors distinctive to each group. Romans 14:3 makes this clear. The key terms concern despising and judging. "The one who eats everything [the strong] must not despise (*exoutheneō*) the one who does not [the weak], and the one who does not eat everything [the weak] must not judge (*krinō*) the one who does [the strong], for God has accepted that person." Without labeling the two groups, Romans 14:10 makes the same appeal: "You, then, why do you judge (*krinō*) your brother or sister? Or why do you despise (*exoutheneō*) your brother or sister? For we will all stand before God's judgment seat."

Paul is concerned that the weak, the more conservative group, not "judge" the strong, the less conservative group. This makes perfect sense. The weak believed that certain days were "sacred" (Rom 14:5) and "special" (Rom 14:6) and some foods were forbidden according to God's law. For them to disregard such laws would be an act of disobedience to God. When they saw other Christians acting in defiance of such laws they were tempted to judge (i.e., condemn) them as being disobedient to God.

The verb "judge" actually occurs seven times in the passage. Along with the commands not to judge in Romans 14:3 and 14:10, Paul asks rhetorically in Romans 14:4, "who are you to *judge* someone else's servant?" And in Romans 14:13 he tells the weak again to "stop *passing judgment* on one another" (both NIV).

The fifth and sixth occurrences appear in Romans 14:5, a verse that uses the verb "judge" in a different sense: "Some *judge* one day to be better than another, while others *judge* all days to be alike." The weak *judge* one day better than others, in the sense of *considering* it to be better than other days.[5]

The seventh use of *krinō* appears in Romans 14:22, where Paul warns about condemning oneself: "The faith that you have, keep between yourself and God. Blessed is the one who has no reason to *pass judgment* [i.e., condemn] on himself for what he approves."[6]

It seems that Paul has "judging" on his mind. There are three acts of "judgment" in the passage. He uses a play on words that also works in English to reinforce his message and make it more memorable:

1. The weak are not to judge (i.e., condemn) the strong for disregarding God's law about days and food.

2. The weak are free to judge (i.e., consider) one day more special than another.

3. The weak and the strong are not to judge (i.e., condemn) themselves.

Paul is just as concerned about the behavior of the strong as the weak. The strong are the less conservative group, taking a less strict line on the application of Jewish food and Sabbath laws. Paul tells them not to "despise" the weak, the more conservative group. Once

---

5. See NIV and HCSB, which translate *krinō* as "consider" in Rom 14:5.

6. Cf. NIV: "So whatever you believe about these things keep between yourself and God. Blessed are those who do not *condemn* themselves by what they approve."

again he is spot-on when it comes to the social psychology of the situation. From their point of view, the strong would easily have regarded the weak as not taking the freedom of the gospel seriously enough and of merely being wedded to their cultural background. Most of the weak were probably former Jews, and to make matters worse there would have been examples of Jewish Christians who no longer kept Sabbath and food laws, such as Paul himself and probably Priscilla and Aquila (compare Rom 16:3). It would only be natural for the strong to look down on the weak.

The verb in question, *exoutheneō*, is translated variously Romans 14:3, 10 as "despise" (NRSV, ESV), "treat with contempt" (NIV), and "look down on" (HCSB). It is used elsewhere in the New Testament in terms of the self-righteous "looking down" on everyone else (Luke 18:9) and of Jesus being "ridiculed" by Herod and the soldiers at his trial (Luke 23:11). Clearly it is not behavior of which the early Christians approved.

According to our simple mirror reading of Romans 14–15, the two parties in dispute were failing to accept each other as being in good standing before God, and they were probably cut off from each other socially. The more conservative group was upset that some Christians were disobeying what they regarded as clear prohibitions from God's Word and was tempted to condemn them accordingly. The less conservative group was tempted to see those still keeping what they regarded as obsolete commands as narrow-minded and was tempted to despise them and treat them with contempt.

Sometimes the distance between our day and Paul's can be considerable. In this case, Paul's insight into the conflict in the Roman church is uncannily current. Sadly, in my experience, the same dynamic often plays out along similar lines when Christians squabble over disputable matters today. A recent example concerns a matter of conduct in connection with a certain biblical command. One group understood the command as a simple and binding prohibition and, in the discussion on social media, sometimes condemned the other group as disobedient to God. The other group saw the command in question differently, with a narrower application, and some responded spitefully, despising the more conservative group. Impugning of motives was common in both directions. While many on both sides continued to accept each other, there were clear instances of judging and despising, and some broken relationships.

In the Sermon on the Mount Jesus also warns about judging and despising other believers. In Matthew 7:1 he cautions, "Do not judge, or you too will be judged." And in Matthew 5:22, in his application of the commandment not to murder, he states, "whoever says to his brother, 'Fool!' will be subject to the Sanhedrin. But whoever says, 'You moron!' will be subject to hellfire."

Many could attest to the serious harm that is done when Christians squabble over disputable matters. How can these situations be avoided? Should Christians avoid coming to a firm view on such matters? Should we avoid teaching our views for fear of provoking judgment and loathing? Should we simply vary our practice in different settings? Paul's answers to such questions may surprise you.

PAUL'S INSTRUCTIONS AND HIS REASONS

As we have seen, Paul's basic instruction to those squabbling in Rome over disputable matters is to accept rather than judge or despise one another. In a letter known for its emphasis on the corporate, Paul's appeal in this case is decidedly individual. In response to Christians judging and despising each other, Paul reasons that each person in the conflict is responsible directly to God, an accountability based on the status of all believers as belonging to the Lord Jesus Christ.

In Romans 14:4 Paul asks incredulously of both parties, "Who are you to judge someone else's servant? To their own master, servants stand or fall" (Rom 14:4a NIV). He insists in 14:6 that ultimately each Christian lives as one directly accountable to God. He underscores his point by using the phrase "to the Lord/to God" (both datives of advantage in the Greek): "Whoever regards one day as special does so *to the Lord*. Whoever eats meat does so *to the Lord*, for they give thanks *to God*; and whoever abstains does so *to the Lord* and gives thanks *to God*."

Verse 8a repeats the point with the same pithy phrase: "If we live, we live *for the Lord*; and if we die, we die *for the Lord*." The line of argument is capped off in 14:8b by asserting God's indisputable claim on our lives: "So, whether we live or die, we belong to the Lord." As Paul puts it in 14:22, "the faith that you have [with respect to Jewish scruples of diet and calendar], keep to yourself before God." When we judge or despise another believer on a disputable matter, we are effectively usurping their true ownership and allegiance. In one sense, what they think about such things is none of our business! God will hold them to account.[7]

The weak in Rome may have thought to themselves, "well and good, God will judge those flouting his law for their sin." But, Paul insists, God will not condemn them. Recalling his magisterial exposition of justification by grace through faith in Romans 1–4, Paul insists in 14:4b that "they will stand [on the Day of Judgment], for the Lord is able to make them stand" (NIV). Or in the words of 14:3b, "God has accepted them." We are to "accept" believers with whom we differ (see Rom 14:1; 15:7) because "God has accepted them." The unit closes on the same note: "Accept one another, then, just as Christ has accepted you."

However, we should not conclude that matters about which Christians hold different views are not important; disputable matters are not nonessential matters, at least not for individual believers when they relate to questions of their own conduct. Questions concerning how to behave on the Sabbath and what to eat at meals could hardly be avoided by the early Christians. The Christians in Rome had no choice but to come to some position. Paul acknowledges this when he says in Romans 14:5b that "everyone should be fully convinced in their own mind." He explains that personal convictions are necessary, for "those who have doubts are condemned if they eat, because their eating is not from

---

7. The same point is made in the appeal to unity in Jas 4:11–12, where James appeals to there being one Judge for all believers: "Brothers and sisters, do not slander one another. ... There is only one Lawgiver and Judge, the one who is able to save and destroy. But you—who are you to judge your neighbor?"

faith; and everything that does not come from faith is sin" (Rom 14:23). "Faith" here is confident assurance before God that we are acting in good conscience. All believers are to live with such confident assurance when it comes to matters of conduct.

Paul also makes it clear that Christian leaders are permitted to teach clearly on matters of dispute. In Romans 14:14a, in the midst of a unit in which he insists that each believer must have his or her own conviction before God, he declares his own stance quite openly: "I know and am persuaded by the Lord Jesus that nothing is unclean in itself." But in Romans 14:14b he avers: "Still to someone who considers a thing unclean, to that one it is unclean." Paul is not forcing his own views on the weak. In the HCSB Romans 14:14 is in brackets, suggesting that it is an aside in Paul's main argument. We may teach a position on a disputable matter, but not insistently according to Paul's example; we should teach "in brackets," so to speak.

Romans 15:1-7 introduces another twist in Paul's account of what to do when Christians differ over disputable matters. He shifts his focus from individual responsibility toward God to a communal focus. In Paul's view, at least in the case of the strong, some flexibility may be needed. Speaking to the strong, and including himself, Paul reasons that we may need to vary our practice in certain settings: We are not just "to please ourselves" (Rom 15:1). Rather, "each of us should please our neighbors for their good, to build them up" (Rom 15:2 NIV). In doing so we act in imitation of Christ, who "did not please himself" (Rom 15:3); to say that Christ did not please himself is a striking understatement, given that he gave up his life for others! Not surprisingly, the calls to unity in the New Testament frequently include a call for humility after the example of Christ:

> In humility consider others better than your-
> selves. Each of you should look not only to your
> own interests, but also to the interests of others.
> Your attitude should be the same as that of Christ
> Jesus ... [who] became obedient to death—even
> death on a cross (Phil 2:3-4, 8).

The model of Jesus for Christian living was intro-duced in Romans 8:29 ("those whom God foreknew he also predestined to be *conformed to the image of his Son*, in order that he might be the firstborn within a large fam-ily," NRSV adapted) and implied in Romans 12:1 ("pres-ent your bodies as a living sacrifice" NRSV). In Romans 15:3 Jesus' service and sacrifice for the sake of the weak (see Rom 5:6) become the gold standard for life within the Christian community. Christ's attitude supports the appeal to bear with the weakness of those who are un-able to eat freely or esteem every day. Good theology can never be an excuse for the arrogant disregard of others. In this case, thinking you are right on a disputable mat-ter does not mean that you can always have things your own way.

"Please yourself" is not a Christian sentiment. In Romans 15:1-3 Paul uses the verb "please" (*areskō*) three times: We are "not to *please* ourselves. ... We should all *please* our neighbors for their good, to build them up. For Christ did not *please* himself." He makes the same point in reference to himself in 1 Corinthians 10:33-11:1: "I try to *please* everyone in everything I do, not seeking my own advantage, but that of many, so that they may be saved. Be imitators of me, as I am of Christ." The irony is that even when it comes to matters of personal conviction, we are not free simply to please ourselves.

Paul's big command in the passage appears in Romans 14:19: "Let us then pursue what makes for peace and for mutual upbuilding." The implication is clear: To squabble will lead to strife and demolish the church.

To recap in general terms, from Romans 14:1–15:7 we learn the following:

1. Some matters are disputable.

2. They might concern biblical interpretation.

3. Different backgrounds can lead to certain positions.

4. We must not judge or despise those of a different persuasion, but rather welcome them as fellow servants of Christ.

5. Every believer should come to a firm view before God if the matter concerns their own behavior.

6. Believers may teach on disputable matters, but not insistently.

7. Believers may vary their practice in light of their context, following Christ's example of not pleasing himself.

8. The bottom line on disputable matters is to pursue what makes for peace and for mutual upbuilding.

HIGH STAKES

Paul reinforces his instructions on not squabbling over disputable matters by pointing to three things that will be seriously impaired if the Roman believers do not heed him: the health and happiness of the church, the progress of the gospel, and the glory of God.

To give both sides some perspective, in Romans 14:17 Paul plays down the significance of the food laws and tells the Christians in Rome what is truly important in the kingdom of God: "For the kingdom of God is not food and drink but righteousness and peace and joy in the Holy Spirit" (NRSV) Whereas Paul can speak of the kingdom of God as a future inheritance (as in 1 Cor 6:9-10; 15:50; Gal 5:21), here it is a present reality in the life of Christians (as in 1 Cor 4:20). The character of this life under God's rule is described in terms of "righteousness, peace and joy" inspired by the Spirit. It is no accident that two of these three qualities appear in the fruit of the Spirit in Galatians 5:22 (namely, joy and peace). In 2 Timothy 2:22-23 Paul advises Timothy to avoid "foolish and stupid arguments" and "quarrels" and instead to pursue, among other things, righteousness and peace.[8]

Both "righteousness" and "peace" are used earlier in Romans in connection with justification and reconciliation with God. However, in this context, as Doug Moo argues, they probably have more to do with "relations

---

8. "Flee the evil desires of youth and pursue *righteousness*, faith, love and *peace*, along with those who call on the Lord out of a pure heart. *Don't have anything to do with foolish and stupid arguments*, because you know they produce *quarrels*."

among believers."[9] What counts in the kingdom is right relations in the community—"righteousness"— and harmony and mutual support among believers—"peace." When these two are in place, the result is "joy." "Righteousness, peace and joy" are each manifestations of life in step with the Holy Spirit.[10]

What Paul underscores in Romans 14:17 is ethics arising from the gospel. The three blessings are, in effect, gifts of the Spirit for the eschatological age. And as Moo notes, this summary of the community's life under God's rule is an outworking of his exposition of the gospel in Romans. This can be seen in the use of three similar terms in Romans 5:1-2, "Paul's transitional encapsulation of the argument in chaps. 1-4":[11] "Therefore, since we have been declared *righteous* by faith, we have *peace* with God through our Lord Jesus Christ. Also through Him, we have obtained access by faith into this grace in which we stand, and we *rejoice* in the hope of the glory of God."

What Paul stresses as vitally important in Romans 14:17 is simply the outworking of our justification and reconciliation to God for our corporate life in his kingdom: Being declared righteous with God must lead to *righteousness in human relationships*; finding peace with God must lead to *living at peace with others.* In other

---

9. Douglas J. Moo, *The Epistle to the Romans*, New International Commentary on the New Testament (Grand Rapids: Eerdmans, 1996), 857.

10. The phrase "in the Holy Spirit," *en pneumatic hagiō,* modifies all three qualities, each being associated in early Jewish and Christian teaching with the new age of the Spirit.

11. Moo, *Romans,* 857.

words, Christian hope and the joy of being right with God should spill over into *the joy of Christian fellowship*. Romans 14:17 indicates that squabbling over secondary matters puts the health and happiness of the church at risk.

Reading beyond Romans 15:7 into the rest of the chapter, it becomes clear that two more things are put in jeopardy when Christians squabble over disputable matters, namely, the progress of the gospel and the glory of God. In Romans 15:8 and following, Paul transitions from discussing disputable matters to declaring his purpose and agenda as an apostle of Jesus Christ. Paul's driving purpose is to proclaim Christ so that the Gentiles would come to faith in Christ and bring praise to God. Grace was given to Paul (Rom 15:15) for him to become "a minister of Christ Jesus to the Gentiles in the priestly service of the gospel of God" (Rom 15:16 NRSV).

For Paul's mission to succeed he needs the Roman Christians, both Jews and Gentiles, to accept one another and not to squabble, so that with one mind and voice they might glorify God (Rom 15:6). Paul's ultimate purpose in dealing with the quarrels in the churches in Rome is not to "smooth things over"; it is that "the Gentiles might glorify God" (Rom 15:9; compare 15:6, 7). Romans 15:7 makes it clear that sorting out certain ethical problems will achieve this purpose: "Accept one another ... in order to bring glory to God." Four Old Testament quotations in Romans 15:9-12 reiterate the goal of Gentiles praising God along "with his people." United churches are a precondition for the effective proclamation of the gospel to the glory of God.

WHICH MATTERS ARE DISPUTABLE?

Clearly there is much at stake when it comes to behaving well when Christians differ over disputable matters. However, how do we know when a matter is disputable and when it is beyond dispute? The New Testament does not provide us with lists for the two categories. Rather, we must rely on wisdom and discernment, as is so often the case in Christian living.[12]

On the one occasion that Paul does label something of "first importance," he is speaking of the gospel of the death and resurrection of Christ (1 Cor 15:1 and following). So according to this text, matters beyond dispute are gospel issues. Presumably, disputable matters are nongospel issues, and Christians sometimes use this nomenclature today. However, we should be cautious in applying this categorization: The gospel is such a profound and precious message that we must take care not to conclude that our formulation of that message is the only way in which it can be expressed. Sometimes disagreements occur when two groups are saying the same thing in different ways. We must beware of "repeat-after-me" theological discussions. Even in the New Testament the various authors have their own ways of saying things.

Part of the problem for so-called nongospel issues is that those who take a more conservative view, like the Christians in Rome who adhered to Jewish food and Sabbath laws, typically regard the issue in question as

---

12. The chapters by Malone, Bird, and Bezzant in this volume touch on this issue.

a matter of obedience to God's Word. In such cases, we must remember Paul's teaching about putting ourselves in the position of judging another servant of Christ, and be careful not to exaggerate the significance of the matter at hand. Many issues of Christian practice are questions for the leadership in a church or Christian organization and not necessarily for every member. This includes things like baptism, church government, the role of women, and the like. While it is vital to come to a firm position if the matter concerns your own behavior, many times my own view is purely "academic" if I am not one of the people responsible for the policy of the group to which I belong.

One question to ask to determine whether something is a disputable matter is whether there is disagreement about it among Christian teachers in good standing who believe in the authority of Scripture. Some might wonder, "But how do I know whether someone has based their position on the Bible or on something else?" The answer is to listen to what they say about why they hold their position. We must resist impugning motives; only God knows the heart. It is possible that someone holds their position because of special pleading and rationalization rather than reading the Bible faithfully, but we must not rush to such conclusions.

Finally, it is worth asking ourselves how we came to our own positions. In the case of the Christians in Rome, their backgrounds and social circles seem to have played a role. You only have to recognize that matters of dispute differ markedly at different times and places to realize that culture is often a major factor. The desire to belong to certain groups can lead to "groupthink," the demonizing of those who think differently in the pursuit of group harmony. Paul's goal of peace and mutual edification (Rom 14:19) is meant to extend beyond our immediate circles.

CONCLUSION

With respect to disputable matters, in Romans 14–15 Paul stresses the need for personal convictions, flexibility, not judging or despising those who disagree, and the goal of peace and edification. As it turns out, the theological foundations of his teaching on disputable matters are remarkably profound. Doctrine matters, especially when it comes to disputable matters. Paul appeals to the lordship of Christ, the imitation of Christ, justification by faith, and the work of the Spirit in the kingdom of God. To behave badly will damage the health and happiness of the church, impede the progress of the gospel, and diminish the glory of God.

CHAPTER 4

WHEN DO WE DIVIDE?

The Johannine Letters on Love and Separation

Michael F. Bird

INTRODUCTION

Kenny Rogers, in his song "The Gambler," famously says, "You gotta know when to hold 'em, know when to fold 'em, know when to walk away, and know when to run." Such a line could easily summarize the problems faced by many congregations who are part of denominations where the leadership is basically heterodox and has rejected—often with a degree of pride—the historic confession of the church. Members of such churches routinely face ridicule, punitive actions, interference, litigation, and marginalization by denominational henchmen for daring to profess that old-time religion. Such congregations or networks then face the difficult question of whether to stay and endure, stay and fight, leave with nothing, or try to leave with their buildings. Let me say that I've experienced firsthand the plight of those in Church of Scotland and the Anglican

Communion who have been faced with difficult choices in this matter: whether to stay or to leave.

I confess that I have genuine sympathy for those who choose to leave. The fact is that some churches have become ideationally vacuous, which is to say that many denominations have no prescriptive theological beliefs, and members and officers of the church can quite literally believe any nonsense they like. One could believe, for instance, that an intergalactic space chimp called "Bob" flew to earth on an interstellar falafel, preached a message of tolerance and eco-care to the people of Earth, was beaten to death by Lebanese llamas in Lesotho, but if you do a chicken dance and say "wobble bobble squabble," one day Bob will return to take you to his home planet of Blisstonia. In some cases, the differences in theology are so vast that one can scarcely even speak of holding to the same religion. The only basis for remaining together has nothing to do with a shared faith, common worship, theological confession, or a similar experience. The only basis for unity is nothing more than pensions and property. Let us remember, as well, that the Bible does have a category for "heresy" and for "idolatry" and repeatedly advocates disciplining those who lead God's people into blatant idolatry, gross immorality, or grievous error. Paul could say to the Roman churches,

> Now I exhort you, brothers, to look out for those who cause dissensions and temptations contrary to the teaching which you learned, and stay away from them. For such people do not serve our Lord Christ, but their own stomach, and by smooth

speech and flattery they deceive the hearts of the unsuspecting (Rom 16:17–18 LEB).

Could it be that schism is necessary for the integrity of the gospel, the continuing holiness of the church, and the promotion of the church's mission to the world? Perhaps so!

But then again I have a lot of antipathy toward calls for schism. For a start, the Holy Catholic Church is already divided between Catholic, Greek Orthodox, Eastern Orthodox, Anglican, and Protestant churches. Within Protestantism itself there are more than thirty thousand denominations. We need another denomination like we need another Babylonian captivity. The current trend of abandoning the denominational ship to go and plant a flurry of independent inner-city churches with a missional ethos might seem like a great solution, but what it gains in freedom it clearly sacrifices in terms of unity and catholicity. The whole concept of "independent churches" is an oxymoron, like "military intelligence" or "fried ice." Justifying separatism with appeals to spiritual unity is a cop-out, since Christians are called to express their spiritual unity in physical and embodied realities of life together, even with all its complications and hassles. I once heard of a denominational leader who wrote in a church's official magazine that unity was overrated. It left me scratching my head and wondering whether Jesus' words "that they all may be one, just as you" are overrated (John 17:21 LEB). Or what about Paul's words, "Brothers, rejoice, be restored, be encouraged, be in agreement, be at peace, and the God of love and peace will be with you" (2 Cor

13:11 LEB) and "being eager to keep the unity of the Spirit in the bond of peace" (Eph 4:3 LEB)? So could it be that while schism happens, it is never justified and should never be pursued as a course of action? Perhaps so!

We must remember that our problems are not entirely new. The early church was not immune to problems of divisions, factions, and schisms. Quite expectedly the New Testament authors have a lot to say about the matter. According to Michael Thompson:

> Some of the strongest words of condemnation in the New Testament are reserved for those whose actions harm and bring discord and divisions among God's people (such as Matt 18:6; Luke 17:1 and following; 1 Cor 3:17; 2 Pet 2:1–3). These teachings should cause those who would innovate at the expense of church unity to ponder carefully whether their action is truly obedient, much less "progressive" or "prophetic." It should likewise make anyone considering leading others away from the church in response to reflect on the danger of tearing apart the visible body of Christ.[1]

So schism is quite a serious matter in biblical teaching and not one to be taken lightly. Therefore, in light of the tension and angst that many have about staying or leaving in troublesome circumstances, the aim of this study is to look at the topic of schism from a biblical perspective. Specifically, I will engage the topic in light of the letters of John, since these letters have a lot to

---

1. Michael B. Thompson, *When Should We Divide* (Ridley Hall, CA: Grove, 2004).

say about division and church life. This will lead us to a biblically informed view about schism and whether the responsible option in church disputes is hold 'em, fold 'em, walk away, or run!

IMPERATIVE OF LOVE

We have to start with the ecclesiastical vision of the Johannine letters, since that shapes the theological context in which church life exists. Love is foundational to John's vision for the church, its theology and practice. Love is absolutely central to the ethical vision of the Johannine letters. The exhortations are replete with commands to love others. Hence the words of the Elder: "We know that we have passed over from death to life because we love the brothers. The one who does not love remains in death" (1 John 3:14 LEB); "We have come to know love by this: that he laid down his life on behalf of us, and we ought to lay down our lives on behalf of the brothers" (1 John 3:16 LEB); and "Little children, let us not love with word or with tongue, but in deed and truth" (1 John 3:18 LEB). These words exposit themes found in the Fourth Gospel about love being the surest test for discipleship (especially John 13). The Elder informs his audience that love is a sign of receiving salvation. Christian love is meant to be an imitation of love that is displayed from God through Christ to believers. Ultimately, love is meant to be expressed in action and not in empty slogans or good intentions. The discourse on love reaches a poignant climax in the latter half of the epistle:

Dear friends, let us love one another, because love is from God, and everyone who loves has been fathered by God and knows God. The one who does not love does not know God, because God is love. By this the love of God is revealed in us: that God sent his one and only Son into the world in order that we may live through him. In this is love: not that we have loved God, but that he loved us and sent his Son *to be the* propitiation for our sins. Dear friends, if God loved us in this way, we also ought to love one another. No one has seen God at any time. If we love one another, God resides in us and his love is perfected in us. By this we know that we reside in him and he in us: that he has given us of his Spirit. And we have seen and testify that the Father has sent the Son *to be the* Savior of the world (1 John 4:7–14 LEB).

In a nutshell, love is part of the saving reality that God ushers in through the incarnation. Love is the true measure of authentic discipleship. Divine love is meant to be like a ray of light shone down on believers who in turn reflect it on others like living mirrors. Love is both the indicative and imperative of Christian ethics. Love is what God has done for and expects of us. The entire grammar of Christian theology is simply an unpacking of divine love and the profession and practice of love for others.

One could aver from all this that the theologic of divine love in John's understanding does not countenance the possibility of schism. Divine love leads us toward imitation of Christ and never toward separation within the body of Christ. Love is given no criteria, no conditions, no qualifications, and no exception clauses. Love is unconditional, all-encompassing, and never optional—it is commanded. As Thompson states, "We must never lose sight of the fact that the struggle to maintain Christian unity (in the Truth) is itself the first step of love towards others. We do not learn to love people by separating from them."[2] In which case, since schism causes the fracture of loving relationships within the church and the rendering of the body, and marks divorce proceedings within congregations, schism is the very antithesis of walking in love and loving each other.

THE CONFESSION OF CHRIST

It would be wrong to say that the Johannine letters focus entirely on unity at the expense of theology or elevate unity entirely over doctrine. John seamlessly combines the two without any thought or hint of divide (see especially 1 John 3:23). The accentuation of love for others in the Johannine letters is combined with a robust christological affirmation, as demonstrated by John the Elder's appeal to the testimony to Jesus (especially 1 John 1:1–3; 5:6–13)—so much so that love and unity rest on adherence to the theological testimony to Christ's person and work. As Stephen Smalley puts it, "John's vision of the Church of his time, and indeed of all time, was for its unity. He saw this as inseparable from an obedience to Christian truth, and from an active love for

---

2. Ibid., 23.

others: within his community and beyond."[3] The primary affirmations of the Johannine testimony to Christ are as follows.

First is the reality of the incarnation. There is the repeated emphasis that Jesus came "in the flesh," an affirmation that was singularly unsuitable to any docetic tendencies in the churches of Ephesus (1 John 4:2; 2 John 7). The atonement (1 John 2:1–2; 3:16) and even Christ's victory over evil (1 John 3:8) are linked to the incarnation. John minces no words when he sets a criterion by which true faith and antifaith can be discerned— specifically, confession of the enfleshing of God the Son in his human life:

> By this you know the Spirit of God: every spirit that confesses Jesus Christ has come in the flesh is from God, and every spirit that does not confess Jesus is not from God, and this is the *spirit* of the antichrist, *of* which you have heard that it is coming, and now it is already in the world (1 John 4:2–3 LEB).

Jesus is the Son of God, and Father and Son mutually indwell each other (1 John 4:15). Jesus is also the source of sharing in divine life and the divine being as he himself shares in God's own life and being: "And we are in him who is true by being in his Son Jesus Christ. He is the true God and eternal life" (1 John 5:20 NIV).

---

3. Stephen S. Smalley, "The Johannine Community and the Letters of John," in *A Vision for the Church: Studies in Early Christian Ecclesiology*, ed. M. Bockmuehl and M. Thompson (Edinburgh: T&T Clark, 1997), 104.

Second is the place of Jesus as the climax of Israel's story. The Jesus of the Johannine Letters is not a heavenly redeemer who fell out of heaven in some seemingly random descent. To the contrary, he comes as the climax to Israel's history, a climax indicated by John's emphatic declaration that Jesus is the *christos* or the Messiah. Confession of Jesus as the Messiah is proof that one is fathered by God and even loves God (1 John 5:1–2).

It would seem that John was fighting a battle on two or more fronts. First, in a Jewish context, profession of Jesus as the Messiah was a stumbling block to Jews and arguably led to the expulsion of many members of the Johannine network of churches from local synagogues. However, John would have no compromise or retreat on this point. Jesus' identity as Messiah remains the rubric of the Church's faith, and its negation would require a wholesale revision of Jesus' teaching and identity. Second, in a Hellenistic context, Jesus is not willing to venerate leaders by having them become so divine as to be unhuman. John will not give quarter to those who want to deny the humanity of Christ because it would be the equivalent of sawing off the branch one is sitting on. Perhaps John knew well, as Athanasius would emphasize some centuries later, that only that which is assumed can be redeemed. Jesus can only be an advocate and sacrifice of atonement if he is fully divine and fully human.

THE PAINFUL AND INEVITABLE PROCESS OF SCHISM

The Johannine letters are brutally honest about the realities of divisions and separation within churches.

The issue comes to a head in the famous passage of 1 John 2:19: "They went out from us, but they did not really belong to us. For if they had belonged to us, they would have remained with us; but their going showed that none of them belonged to us" (NIV). If five years in Scotland taught me anything it is that the history of interpretation of this verse is the history of Presbyterianism in Scotland and America. In context, John refers allusively to a decisive division that has recently taken place within the cluster of churches with whom he is associated. He locates this division within the wider context of a struggle with the world and against the various antichrists whose entrance marks the presence of the last days. John's explanation for what transpired in the torrid affair is that the dissenters did not really belong to the community. It would seem that the faith of the dissenters was transitory, illusory, and falsified proving itself to be fleeting in the end. Of course, the phenomenon that John is describing is not unique. Jesus himself taught about various types of pseudo-faith in the parable of the Sower (see Mark 4:1–20). Paul could also make forthright denunciations of anyone preaching a different Jesus or a different gospel (1 Cor 11:4–9; Gal 1:6–9; 2:11–14). An impassioned polemic characterizes Jude and 2 Peter as being against the unwholesome recasting of Christian belief by people and their followers who bend the truth to suit their own appetites.

John specifies and intensifies his warnings in his letter to the "chosen lady" to make sure she does not receive the deceivers and antichrists with their false teaching. She is warned not to do so because it gives the intruders a foothold in her household and means risking the reward she has worked for (2 John 8), drifting away from the teaching of Christ (2 John 9). Anyone who welcomes them shares in their work (2 John 11), so it is imperative that they not be shown customary hospitality (2 John 10). It really is a case of not letting false teachers get even a foot in the door.

It would seem that, for John, schism is never sought but is simply the result of what happens when truth and error are brought into close proximity, like the natural separation of oil and water. As Colin Kruse points out:

> It is certainly true that 1 John highlights the evil of schism and doctrinal division, something which is always painful when it occurs in the Christian community. It is also true that Christians can be quite unloving, unable to recognise the limited scope of their own understanding of the truth, and therefore much too quick to brand others as "antichrists." There is a great need for humility in matters about which Christians differ. However, at times erroneous teaching which is plainly at variance with the truth of the gospel has to be named, and its origins exposed.[4]

While John urges his audience to walk in love and to follow the example of Jesus, it seems that he is not willing to compromise the christological foundations of the church's faith for the sake of unity. When it comes to the person and work of Jesus Christ, John the Elder brooks no rivals, suffers no fools, gives no quarter, and

---

4. Colin G. Kruse, *The Letters of John* (Grand Rapids: Eerdmans, 2000), 102.

refuses to negotiate the non-negotiable elements of the church's testimony to Jesus. The danger is that some may be opposed to the church's claims about Jesus, the so-called "antichrists" (1 John 2:18, 22; 4:3; 2 John 7), and preach a different Jesus, to use Pauline language (2 Cor 11:4). Such persons may leave, and their leaving may not necessarily be a bad thing because it proves that they possess a different identity, a different system of values, and even a different faith than those who profess that Jesus is the Christ, who came in the flesh, by water and by blood, and is a propitiation for the sins of the world. In such cases, we might infer that the true measure of any group claiming to represent the body of Christ is its imitation of Jesus Christ in their love-ethics and their theological representation of Jesus Christ in symbol and story.

WHEN PUSH COMES TO SHOVE

The question is, should the good guys ever do the leaving? Should they initiate the divorce proceedings, as it were? The letters of John give no indication that this should ever be the case. John envisages the churches continuing in the faith, acting in love, and holding to the teaching of Jesus. That said, John is hardly addressing how churches should act in every conceivable scenario. John's exhortations provide a set of principles for maintaining love and faith within the body when, assuming the best, orthodoxy is still the position of the majority. They do not, however, provide guidance for every possible scenario that might emerge, such as how to deal with a presbytery filled with elders who have a low christology or a bishop who rejects the necessity of the atonement for salvation. To continue in an unyielding profession of the gospel requires wisdom in tandem with a devout commitment to the unity of the body of Christ. There are no easy answers here.

What we can say with clear biblical warrant is that, as evidenced by the Johannine letters, to preserve the integrity of the faith and the unity of the church, it is sometimes painfully necessary to eject persons who have reached a point where they have capitulated to the world rather than hold fast to the word. That is not to say that persons should be disciplined without due process or rejected over secondary matters. But where the christological confession of the church is at stake—confession pertaining to the person and work of Christ—there are grounds for warnings and then for discipline against those who tinker with the Church's teaching about Jesus Christ. We can infer from the thrust of John's message about love and faith that schism is painful and wrong, and while schism should not be pursued as a deliberate matter of course, it can be an inevitable result of standing for the truth of the gospel.

In closing, I'm reminded of a story about an American bishop who was feeling pressure to lead his diocese out of the Episcopal Church. He had worked hard himself to remain in and tried to convince his priests and wardens that they had a duty to remain and to testify to the truth. However, the denomination's moral decline and brazen acceptance of outright heresy left many feeling betrayed, angry, and insisting that they had to leave at the first possible opportunity. The bishop consulted with one of the world's leading Anglican churchmen, the great Reverend John Stott. Stott himself had faced his own challenges with heterodoxy in the Church of England and, despite an infamous confrontation with Martin Lloyd Jones over the subject in 1966, he and others had elected to stay. Stott's reply to the bishop was simple yet profound: "Why should you have to leave, you've got the gospel on your side." In the course of intramural conflicts, one should be willing to be thrown out for standing for the truth when in a confessional minority. But one should never walk out. That premise seems to be congruent with the witness of John.

CHAPTER 5

DISPUTABLE MATTERS IN PROTESTANT HISTORY

How to Express Christian Freedom

Rhys Bezzant

FREEDOM TO BE FLEXIBLE FOR THE SAKE OF MISSION

It was in 1991 at a meeting of the International Fellowship of Evangelical Students (IFES) in Chicago, immediately after the fall of communism and at the end of the Cold War, that delegates debated some difficult matters of mission. For example, the leadership of IFES had asked the student movement in the Federal Republic of Germany to integrate with the student movement in the former socialist German Democratic Republic. In South Africa, Nelson Mandela had been released from prison in 1990, and many of the acts legislating apartheid had been repealed in 1991, so IFES had asked black and white movements in that country to be integrated. Less dramatically, the growth in numbers of Chinese students on Canadian campuses, reflecting the growth of the Chinese diaspora in the country more generally, led to the Canadian Inter-Varsity Fellowship asking IFES for permission to form a Chinese student movement in parallel with its English-speaking and French-speaking movements. After all, there were two parallel student movements in Switzerland, one for the French- and one for the German-speaking cantons. Many member movements in the course of this congress saw inconsistency, partiality, or perhaps even racism in the policies of IFES, which had demanded single national organizations in some places but allowed several parallel movements within one country elsewhere. Did these policies reflect sordid opportunism or rather appeal to deeper, unifying theological principles that generated flexibility according to context?

As an Australian delegate at the assembly, I made an effort to defend the ideal of maximizing freedom among the member movements, generated by belief in the gospel, by appeal to convictions concerning disputable matters, sometimes referred to as things indifferent or *adiaphora*. Just as Paul had insisted that Timothy be circumcised for his ministry, though Titus was not, so I argued that in our day some student ministries might be expected to be shaped by a national agenda and others by more local agendas according to what might best serve the advance of the gospel in that place. In South Africa, where suspicion and oppression had separated out the races, the beauty of the gospel might best be seen through racially reconciled fellowships. On the other hand, in Canada, where no such suspicion had been part of the story of campus ministry, the gospel might best be served by targeting student populations according to linguistic distinctions. Their separated ministries had grown out of trust, not hatred. There was no single right or wrong way of constructing campus ministry. Both could find biblical support, for there is wisdom in shaping ministry structures or goals according to mission opportunities, cultural conditions, theological needs, or pastoral deficits. These debates remind us in stark fashion that healthy cooperation in ministry at local, national, or even international levels may involve recognition that there is room for disagreement on some matters even while holding fast to others of central importance.

This chapter builds on the others in this book by trusting the reader is familiar with the detailed exegesis of texts that give permission to allow freedom in the Christian church on certain matters of dispute. By defining *adiaphora* as those beliefs or practices that are neither prescribed nor proscribed in the Scriptures, but assuming that there are normative beliefs and practices that the doctrine of salvation by grace does entail, it is my goal to offer some wider historical and systematic reflections on matters indifferent, from the sixteenth, seventeenth, and eighteenth centuries, concluding with some personal reflections on present ministry challenges in my context. Much can be learned from Christian history on how Christians might learn to disagree, and though this chapter will treat Anglican and Puritan disagreements as a rich case study, we could also profit from inquiry into Baptist or Presbyterian ecclesiology. On the one hand, we find in the Bible texts that warn that "those who do such things will not inherit the kingdom," or encouragements to "be of one mind," suggesting that our freedom is limited. But, on the other hand, we come across texts acknowledging that for some a matter not proceeding from faith will be sin, though for another that same matter will not be sinful, according to the conscience of the one undertaking it. Contextual application and freedom of conscience are held high in a Protestant view of the mission of the church, while recognizing that claims to spiritual freedom can easily be conflated with the culture in which the claims are made.

FREEDOM OF CONSCIENCE IN SIXTEENTH-CENTURY THEOLOGY

The freedom of the Christian to resist external authority was an emotionally loaded debate from the earliest days of the Reformation, when Martin Luther wrote his famous 1520 tract under the same name. To defend this existential commitment, Luther attacked both the understanding of penance and indulgences that failed to provide pastoral balm to the anxious soul, and the priesthood that promoted them. Famously, he had come to the profound realization that the righteousness of God in Romans 1:16 was not the bleak and universal *demand* of God for a moral life that was unattainable but rather the intrusive and surprising *gift* of forgiveness from God through Jesus Christ to the individual by faith. Philosophically speaking, he inclined towards voluntarism, asserting the freedom of God to work within the creation in unpredictable ways. This was gospel contrasted starkly with Old Testament law.

With justification as the material principle of the Reformation, and appeal to scriptural authority (not ecclesiastical tradition, papal decrees, ecumenical councils, or scholastic theology) as the formal principle, points of leverage had been established to begin to reform the late medieval church of Germany. This strategy was effectively focused on returning the church to its christological center. Luther was not concerned or, given political realities, perhaps not even able, to reform the church in root and branch. He left many matters untouched and allowed liberty to bishops or even princes to pursue reform as they saw fit. He hoped that in time the reforming momentum that he had achieved at the center would wash through to the edges as well. Despite Anabaptist protestations, freedom was not to be hurried. The freedom of the Christian's conscience in the face of totalizing ecclesiastical realities, and the freedom of the leaders of the church to renew its life according to contextual political realities, meant that *adiaphora* were assumed in his theological understanding of reform.

The Frenchman John Calvin, a second-generation Reformer ministering as an exile in Geneva, took up much of the Lutheran agenda but asked a different question. For him, it was not how we can find a gracious God, but rather where can we find the true church, that animated his ministry. An ecclesiological question about the authority of the Mass, not an existential question concerning assurance, was the starting place for reform in France. It was the book of Hebrews rather than Paul's letter to the Romans that sparked the ill-fated French Reformation.[1] Calvin defended the freedom

---

1. B. Cottret, *Calvin: A Biography*, trans. M. W. McDonald (Grand Rapids: Eerdmans, 2000), 71–73.

of the Christian from unwarranted priestly interference by arguing that just as the Christian's conscience is not bound by the Old Testament law, or ceremonies that are now obsolete, so, by an argument from greater to lesser, the Christian's conscience must not be bound by any other external matters, including the sacerdotal priesthood. Calvin began with christological assumptions as Luther had, but he pressed them further. Calvin didn't just regard matters as indifferent because they were not at the center of soteriological concern but went on to explain how matters on the perimeter of Christian obedience should be interpreted theologically:

> We must now discuss Christian freedom. He who proposes to summarize gospel teaching ought by no means to omit an explanation of this topic. For it is a thing of prime necessity. ... Freedom is especially an appendage of justification and is of no little avail in understanding its power. ... Unless this freedom be comprehended, neither Christ nor gospel truth, nor inner peace of soul, can be rightly known.[2]

Christian freedom is central to the truth of the gospel, and the gospel cannot be understood unless our freedom in Christ is affirmed. The true Church for Calvin is not just the place where Christ is owned as Savior, freeing us from anxiety and sin, but it is also the domain where he is praised as Lord, ruling his people by his word, the scepter of his reign, denying any place

---

2. John Calvin, *Institutes of the Christian Religion*, ed. J. T. McNeill, trans. F. L. Battles (Louisville: Westminster John Knox, 1960), 3.19.1.

to usurping authority, which would inhibit our freedom as sons and daughters. It is significant that his section on freedom appears directly before his long chapter on prayer in 3.20, for the greatest blessing of Christian experience—direct access to God through the Son and by the Spirit—is only comprehensible when seen as a corollary of our freedom in Christ.

FREEDOM OF CONSCIENCE: AN ANGLICAN CASE STUDY

Defending Christian freedom in small town Germany or Switzerland was difficult, but establishing Christian freedom in a whole kingdom in the sixteenth century involved quite another set of challenges, making the Church of England in the Reformation a rich case study. Spiritual freedom for a whole nation raised significant disagreements of strategy and ends. It wasn't just that the Reformation in England had comprehensive national scope, but according to the great Yale church historian Jaroslav Pelikan, the Anglican Church also consisted of several theological streams: Lutheran in its roots, Reformed in its doctrine, and Catholic in its polity.[3] It should come as no surprise, then, that its formularies recognized *adiaphora* by distinguishing between those things "requisite for salvation" and those that were not (see article 6 of the Thirty-Nine Articles).

This freedom-giving soteriological aspiration was nonetheless set within the traditional threefold order

---

3. Jaroslav Pelikan, *Reformation of Church and Dogma* (1300–1700, The Christian Tradition: A History of the Development of Doctrine (Chicago: University of Chicago Press, 1984), 2.

of ministry of bishops, priests, and deacons to secure stability. Establishing continuity with the polity of the pre-Reformation church recognized the value of historical development and cultural contingencies guiding the growth of the Church after the New Testament, and took a step back from biblical primitivism and its ministry constraints, which would have denied freedom to any model of church structure other than that purportedly plainly seen in the New Testament. Article 19, "Of the Church," boldly states that churches have erred, denying to them irrefragable authority over the conscience of the individual believer and relativizing their power. It further defines a church "as a congregation of faithful men, in which the pure Word of God is preached, and the Sacraments be duly administered according to Christ's ordinance." The definition focuses on the christological center of the Church and importantly makes no mention of the threefold order otherwise so prized by Anglicans as central to their identity. An individual's freedom of conscience is acknowledged, with the recognition that the form of the church does not secure gospel purity.

Article 20, "Of the Authority of the Church," we must similarly parse carefully, for it uses two distinct words in the original Latin (here italicized) to define how the church goes about resolving dispute. It has "*power* to decree Rites or Ceremonies," or to establish discipline in its liturgical life, but it has "*authority* in Controversies of Faith" to adjudicate matters of disputed doctrine. At the heart of Anglican ecclesiology is the distinction between two types of dispute, which require two types of authority to resolve. Not all matters disputed within

the church are of the same order, for some require power and others authority to bring to an end, and they
ought to be treated differently when they emerge in
parish or diocesan life. Matters of contention are dis-
tinguishable by their place in the life of the church and
the role they play relative to other doctrines or practices. Further, in this same article the church is presented
as subordinate in its authority to the Scriptures, which
are the norming norm: "although the Church be a witness and a keeper of Holy Writ, yet, as it ought not to
decree any thing against the same, so besides the same
ought it not to enforce any thing to be believed for necessity of Salvation." To be able to reform the Church
is to allow for appeal to be made to an authority above
the Church, namely the Word, which is the revivifying
center of its life.

Article 32, "Of the Marriage of Priests," asserts the
freedom of the Christian minister to marry or to remain single, no matter whether he is a bishop, priest,
or deacon, and asserts the right of all Christian people
"to marry at their discretion." Furthermore, diverse
"Traditions and Ceremonies" in the church are to be ac-
commodated when expressed in love "for the consciences of the weak brethren," and with respect to due order
according to Article 34, a clear acknowledgement of the
principle of freedom in matters indifferent. And Article
36, most controversially, makes clear that ordinations
since the reign of Edward VI are indeed valid, despite
external political changes under Mary Tudor and then
Elizabeth I: A matter that has been at the forefront of
the church's polity, the nature and validity of holy or-
ders, is here recognized as being something on which

Anglican Christians might charitably disagree. Finally, while Anabaptists in the sixteenth century saw no place whatsoever for the taking of oaths, Anglicans acknowledged them in Article 39 as permissible. Even the shape of the Articles acknowledges the priority of faith (the doctrine of God, his revelation, and salvation in articles 1–18) before the concerns of order (the church and structures of nurture and obedience in articles 19–39), rather than listing areas of debate at that time at the head of the list, which might have been a concrete way of providing Protestant credentials.

The teachings of Luther, Calvin, and the Anglican Reformers all allow room for disagreement within the camp to promote the Christian's freedom of conscience on certain secondary matters. The church is not to be defined mechanically by its ceremonial or by its discipline but by its theological heart, where freedom reigns. The true Church is christologically focused and embraces all those who find their life in union with him. It is not primarily an ecclesiastical structure, for even in the Anglican Church, the threefold order is for the *bene esse*, and not the *esse*, of the church.

COMING FULL CIRCLE: PURITANS ELEVATE THE CHURCH

It has often been said that the agenda of the Reformation was to assert the priority of Augustine's doctrine of grace over his doctrine of the Church. Indeed, the earliest Reformers of the sixteenth century set themselves to reform the Western Roman church, which had implicitly made its own ministry structure the essence of the church, for it was only through the channel of priestly ministration that grace was to be received. It held that without due deference to the papal church, no true faith could exist, for to be in communion with the vicar of Christ was to be in communion with Christ himself. The visceral reaction of the Roman church to attempts at reform in northern Europe was generated by its assumption that true faith should be *dependent on true order*, inverting the Augustinian assumptions of the magisterial Reformers, who were guided by the belief that true faith is *expressed in true order* and not the other way around. While Protestants might fight vociferously for their own understanding of the link between an individual's faith and the structure of the Church, there was nonetheless agreement that the gospel created the Church, for the Word was at its center, and that the gospel could survive in a variety of ecclesiastical settings and was not dependent on them. The Church did not come before the gospel but the other way around.

This view was, however, jeopardized in the seventeenth century with the attempts by some Puritans to create a church pure in polity.[4] Their line of argument ran thus: Any intrusion into the life of the local congregation by an external authority, normally associated with the ministry of a bishop but potentially associated in some minds with the decisions of a presbytery, would necessarily undermine the freedom of that congregation to organize its own life and thereby compromise its worship, by intruding on the marriage relationship between the spouse of Christ, the church, and her lover,

---

4. John von Rohr, "*Extra Ecclesiam Nulla Salus*: An Early Congregational Version," *Church History* 36, no. 2 (1967): 107–21.

the Lord himself. Any outside influence would be adulterous. Only local discipline established by the consensus of church members could secure purity of worship, and ultimately the purity of the gospel itself. In New England, the Puritan project was essentially an errand to secure pure worship, and only congregationalism could achieve this goal. It is with great irony that the Puritans of the Massachusetts Bay Colony had unwittingly committed the Roman Catholic error of making true faith dependent on true order, by asserting that the gospel can only survive in churches with a particular polity and by assuming that the structure of a church is the sine qua non of gospel vitality.

Cyprian, in the third century, had argued that outside of the (Roman) Church there was no salvation. Now the Puritans of New England were saying almost the same thing. While strictly speaking it is no longer possible to be a Puritan in the twenty-first century, for it is no longer viable in the post-Christian West to coordinate the life of the church with the life of the state, nonetheless a similar mind-set can still be found, which inverts the sixteenth-century Protestant order and assumes that for the gospel to survive, let alone thrive, only one way of doing things in the Church can be accepted, or only one structure of church polity or ministry arrangements can secure the purity of gospel proclamation. A caution nonetheless emerges from the eighteenth century, where the Puritan understanding of the church ran up against the new conditions of Enlightenment and empire, challenging the potency of its ecclesiology. In the next section we will see how modernity stimulated new focus in ecclesiology and provided renewed energy to evangelical protest.

FREEDOM AND FLEXIBILITY FROM EVANGELICAL PERSPECTIVE

During the evangelical revivals in the eighteenth century in Germany, Austria, and Britain and its colonies, conservative Protestantism adapted its life to modern conditions. This provoked either new possibilities for renewal within Protestant denominations, which had grown lazy or aridly doctrinaire since the Reformations of the sixteenth century, or new debates concerning the nature of authority, which had hobbled Protestantism from the beginning, and the Anglican church more particularly since the English civil wars of the 1640s and 1650s. Put succinctly, Christian believers redirected their spiritual impatience with the recalcitrance of church institutions to reform their polity toward reconstruction of their own heart and the transposition of theological concerns into an effective key. The evangelical movement, whether revivalist in its frontier or Methodist incarnations, or more nurturing in its Anglican or Lutheran guise, held high the value of vital piety, experimental religion, or personal experience as a way around many of the intractable debates of the seventeenth century. To regenerate the church should begin with regeneration of the individual's heart as a kind of firstfruits of the harvest. Encouraged by Jakob Spener in Germany, small groups of likeminded regenerate believers would function as leaven in the batch to bring new life to the broader congregation.[5] In the journals of George Whitefield, an Anglican clergyman turned itinerant preacher and perhaps the best-known celebrity of his day in the American colonies, the regenerative word would marginalize and possibly transform theological disagreements and create room for greater freedom to acknowledge *adiaphora*:

> Monday, Feb. 27. Went to church, and did as yesterday; and was visited afterwards by two of the Nonconforming Society, who seemed to be Israelites indeed. I exhorted them to love and unity, and not to let a little difference about a few externals occasion any narrow-spiritedness to arise in their hearts.

> Tuesday, March 7. What a pity it is, Christ's seamless coat should be rent in pieces on account of things in themselves purely indifferent.

The rise of itinerancy and the loss of traditional geographic or ecclesiastical boundaries for authority, indeed the valorizing of experience and the promotion of the doctrine of regeneration, together played their part in shaking the church and making it confront the new contingencies of human agency, globalizing culture, the social solvent of capitalism, and changing patterns of discipline. Flexibility was established in ministry at the cost of some traditional structures of authority already losing their raison d'être. Loose associations of

---

5. Philip Jacob Spener, *Pia Desideria*, trans. T. G. Tappert, seminar ed. (Philadelphia: Fortress, 1964).

clergy and laity were proving more effective in releasing ministry energy than either strict episcopal or congregationalist polities had been. Following the Spirit could provide both power and discipline for the task of evangelism and nurture. Freedom in structure to adapt to modern conditions was increasingly seen as healthy for the life of the church.

Indeed, evangelicals grew in influence in the nineteenth and twentieth centuries, collaborating with likeminded believers from other churches across denominational boundaries and in different lands. Appealing to freedom of conscience in matters indifferent, they formed coalitions to fight the scourge of British slavery, to create nondenominational societies in early republican American to make good the promise of a virtuous citizenry as guarantor of liberty against the intrusion of government, and to engage with the new and appalling conditions of the industrial age. It was not only evangelicals who worked for these ends, but they achieved great outcomes through their principled pragmatism on secondary matters. The Evangelical Alliance was formed in Britain in 1846; its legacy is evident today in the World Evangelical Alliance. In their "Practical Resolutions: A Commitment to Relationships," their fundamental affirmations are:

> 1. We welcome as Christian brothers and sisters all who experience the grace of new birth, bringing them to that fear and knowledge of God which is expressed in a life of obedience to His word.

2. We recognize our Christian duty of trust and mutual encouragement to all who serve Christ as Lord, not least to those who conscientiously prefer not to be identified with the same churches, alliances or councils as ourselves.

3. We respect the diversity of culture, experience and doctrinal understanding that God grants to His people, and acknowledge that some differences over issues not essential to salvation may well remain until the end of time.

Commitments like these were born in the Victorian era, when the modern missions movement—itself growing out of evangelical energy and innovation of the eighteenth century—taught Western missionaries how to distinguish between first- and second-order issues. Recognition of *adiaphora* has been a significant factor contributing to the growth of the global church in our own day.

MANAGING DISPUTABLE MATTERS IN THE ANGLICAN CHURCH

Anglican evangelicals find themselves on the horns of a dilemma. They value the stability and sustainability that a well-governed institutional expression of church provides, yet are restless to create fresh expressions and exercise evangelistic entrepreneurial spirit. They rightly set the word of the gospel above the life of the church, a word that brings both order and interruption in its train, and they rejoice in the ministry of the Spirit, which cultivates in us both power and discipline, energy and fruitfulness. We have learned that a commitment to *adiaphora* is both acceptable according to our formularies and healthy for our ministries. We want neither to absolutize the church nor to relegate it to a purely instrumental role in our lives and mission. We want to remain critical of, and committed to, its Anglican forms. This dynamic tension has been one of the greatest gifts that evangelicals have brought to Anglicanism, beginning, for example, with the desire of John and Charles Wesley to remain within its fold to work to sanctify their nation and renew the life of its church in their own day.

This tension exists at the heart of the Anglican Church as a Protestant denomination, for it is grounded in its episcopal order but appropriately does not make of such order any totalizing claims in the Articles, the Ordinal, or in the Book of Common Prayer. All clergy take oaths to uphold this order, but nowhere do they declaim that the threefold order of bishops, priests, and deacons is of the essence of the church. Sixteenth-century English Protestants knew the theological difficulties that would follow if such a position were upheld. It is my contention that this approach by evangelicals to the episcopal polity of the church can function as a paradigm in other areas of church life and for those Christians who are not Anglican as well: We gladly submit where church practices can be seen as entailments of the gospel (even when we might be unconvinced of some of the details of the argument), though we rightly resist when the gospel is said to stand or fall on the basis of a certain understanding of polity. As Luther averred, it is the doctrine of justification that has that place alone. Living within a church structure that is impaired, or not our own preference for polity, does not invalidate our gospel preaching nor our gospel freedom, as long as our conscience is not constrained from offering gospel critique. Appeal to the existence of disputable matters ought not to be seen as incompatible with any particular polity, or as a weakness in our church, for it means setting the content of the faith above any time-bound expression of it.

A way of resolving disputable matters can be derived from the book of Acts. The Gamaliel principle is offered to us in Acts 5, which essentially advocates the policy of "wait and see"—not all disagreements have to be resolved now. Indeed, churches with their roots in the sixteenth-century reformations ought to be expert in allowing time to help them see what God will bring from a difficult situation or debate. We must be patient with each other when appeals to freedom in matters indifferent are claimed. On the other hand, the Jerusalem Council described in Acts 15 was required to make a decision concerning the inclusion of the Gentiles in the church of God and, not being able to wait any longer, gave minimal direction to the leaders of churches in relation to contentious matters to avoid giving offense (even when taking offense cannot be avoided). Sometimes a decision just has to be made for the institutional integrity of the denomination, but it ought to provide maximum freedom to not give offense to those for whom the decision is difficult to receive. Love has to be careful not to insist on its own way.

The experience of Anglicans in Australia in recent years has witnessed legal appeal to formal forums of conflict resolution to establish overdue outcomes, especially in the matter of the ordination of women. These processes have, of course, been difficult for many. We should therefore be working all the harder to develop and to avail ourselves of other avenues of trust building and consensus forming, through which seemingly intractable disagreements can be faced. Synod is a clumsy forum for sensitive debates, and local deaneries might not be much more effective in many places. The importance of patiently growing relationships is especially pertinent when we acknowledge the generational and psychological preferences of church leaders born since the 1970s, who are less denominationally attached and more relationally open. Inclusion has been their educational and social experience, and they affirm pluralism not necessarily for its own sake but rather to have their voice heard. In many corners of our church, we preach inclusion but practice generational denial.

Having acknowledged the historical place and theological value of *adiaphora* within the Protestant tradition, it is finally worth acknowledging the opportunity that spiritual ecumenism, rather than institutional uniformity or councils, might provide in response to disagreements, and thereby replicate what is increasingly the practice in ecumenical exchanges between churches and communions. This model of engagement suits well the temperament and traditions of evangelicals, who almost instinctively are attracted toward other believers who prioritize familiar spiritual values and practice familiar spiritual disciplines. Common prayer among priest and people is at the heart of our Reformation assumptions, which might yet have renewed application in our own day. Indeed, celebrating others' gospel fruit in conversions and growth toward Christian maturity, no matter which party one belongs to, may well relativize our angst in matters indifferent and promote reforming ideals in ways we haven't yet imagined. It has to be worth a try.

CHAPTER 6

REMAPPING THE CHURCH

Migration, Transnationality, and the Future Church

Peter J. Leithart

Once there were no denominations. Once the Church was not mappable into three great "families" of churches—Catholic, Protestant, and Orthodox.

Once there was just "the Church," then East and West, then, over several centuries, the crazy quilt of churches we know today. Greek and Latin churches diverged from each other from the earliest centuries, but they remained officially united until the mutual anathemas of 1054. Prior to the sixteenth century, what became Europe knew only the "Latin" or "Western" church, which was catholic and centered in Rome but was not the Roman Catholic Church. As the Great Schism created "Catholicism" and "Orthodoxy," so the Protestant Reformation produced not only "Lutheran" and "Reformed" and "Anglican" churches, but also founded the Catholic Church as a distinct Christian body. The teeming varieties of Protestantism have all emerged since the sixteenth century.

Denominationalism was not lurking under the sur-
face, waiting to pop out when Martin Luther catalyzed
it. The three "families" did not exist in seminal form pri-
or to the various fissures that produced them. The distinctions and groupings, the territorial boundaries, the
liturgical and doctrinal differences, all the topographi-
cal clues and cues by which we map the Christian world
today, had to be *created*.

Whatever was "once" true but is *not* true any longer is contingent, by definition. "Once" is a signal that
whatever is under consideration is not a design feature. Our mapping of the Church into three clusters of
churches has emerged over the course of a thousand
years of CZhurch history. It is in no way essential to
the Church, as Jesus and the Spirit, the Scriptures and
sacraments, are of the essence of the Church. Ecclesial
maps have changed in the past. They will change again.
The Church as we know it had to be mapped, and it
is remappable.

Edit that: It is not re*mappable*. It *is being* remapped
before our eyes, if we open our eyes to see it. Or, edit
again: It *has been* remapped, while many of us had our
heads down and our eyes fixed obsessively on the frequently petty travails of our own denominations.[1]

When the World Missionary Conference met in
Edinburgh in 1910, *no* representatives from Africa, Latin

---

1. As Philip Jenkins has pointed out, this is literally true:
The demographic and geographic center of Christianity is in Asia,
Africa, and Latin America. See especially *The Next Christendom:
The Coming of Global Christianity* (Oxford: Oxford University
Press, 2011).

America, or the Pacific Island churches were invited.[2] Today, no international conference would fail to include many leaders from these continents, but our mental routines too often run along rails that were already flecked with rust in 1910. It has been a long time since Will Herberg could accurately summarize the religious life of the United States as *Protestant Catholic Jew*. It has been a long time since we could accurately summarize the Church as *Protestant Catholic Orthodox*. Our maps are badly out of date, and it is time to notice and to ask what it might mean.

I'll begin with two illustrative vignettes of the new, burgeoning African Christian movements that fall outside our habitual trifold taxonomy. These movements have been examined and reported on elsewhere, more thoroughly than I can do here. This essay is a pointing finger: "Look over here!" I want to say. "What do we make of *that*? How does it force us to change our ecclesial habits? And what opportunities does it offer for our pursuit of unity?" The sheer existence of these movements poses an intellectual and practical challenge to European, North American, and Australian churches, but their impact is deeper than simply forcing us to modulate from a triple to a quadrilateral classification. Later, I examine how immigrant African churches in the United States might affect not only the African churches themselves but American Christianity, especially how the new immigrant churches might contest and modify America's denominational form of Christianity. I do not

<hr />

2. Scott W. Sunquist, *Understanding Christian Mission: Participation in Suffering and Glory* (Grand Rapids: Baker Academic, 2013), 118.

focus on the United States because I think it is the most important laboratory of the future church. America is even less of the essence of the Church than "Orthodoxy" or "Lutheran" or "Roman Catholic" are. I turn to North America partly because it is the world I know and partly because its denominational system has been the paradoxical source of much of both the vibrancy and the volatility of Christianity during the past two centuries. If immigrant churches have the potential to cause some fraying of American denominationalism, the fabric will likely unravel elsewhere as well.

The Swedish Mission Covenant Church entered the Belgian Congo in 1909. Despite early successes in the first decades of the twentieth century, the missionaries were dissatisfied with the results. They were making converts, but conversion was making little difference in the lives of new believers. Leaders of the mission gathered for a retreat in January 1947 for prayer and soul searching.

During the retreat, the mission's head, John Magnusson, preached a sermon on John 3:16 and afterward invited others to pray. A student at the seminary in Ngouedi, Raymond Buana Kibongi (also spelled Kibongui), rose to pray for the seminary, which was, he claimed "rotting from within." Shaking, Kibongi cried, "Jesus, make me your servant. Jesus, calm me down, calm me down," until he became too exhausted to stand.

The meeting sparked a revival. As Ogbu Kalu recounts, "people confessed their 'kintantu,' envy or hatred, and poor relationships across racial lines, and they changed dramatically. Others realized their Christian dullness and the low level of church attendance and poor prayer lives in the school and improved."[3] Others were caught up in "the ecstasy of the cross," feeling pain in their palms, and fell to the ground, stiff as corpses. Prophets, *ngunza*, visited the retreat, drank the Spirit, and spread the revival's zeal throughout the Congo. Villages touched by the revival were transformed. Kibongi reflected, "Just as hard iron can only melt in fire, so the black man's stone heart can only be melted in the all consuming fire of the ecstasy."[4]

Kibongi lived until 1998, and in the decades after 1947 he was instrumental in forming the Evangelical Church of Congo, a catholic effort that included white and black churches. In 1950 he became the first head of the *Conseil des Eglises Chretiennes au Congo*. Brazzaville Pentecostals still think of themselves as "revival churches," tracing

---

3. Ogbu Kalu, *African Pentecostalism: An Introduction* (Oxford: Oxford University Press, 2008), 45. Kalu tells the same story more briefly in Hugh McLeod, ed., *Cambridge History of Christianity*, vol. 9, *World Christianities, c. 1914–2000* (Cambridge: Cambridge University Press, 2006), 211–12. A few more details are found at http://www.dacb.org/stories/congo/ndoundou_daniel.html. It is remarkably difficult to find information about Kibongi, and I am heavily reliant on Kalu's account. The main account is Carl Sundberg, *Conversion and Contextual Conceptions of Christ: A Missiological Study among Young Converts in Brazzaville, Republic of Congo* (Swedish Institute of Missionary Research, 2000), unfortunately unavailable to me.

4. Quoted in Kalu, *African Pentecostalism*, 46.

their history back to Kibongi's ecstasy and his remarkable, lifelong ministry.[5]

The Evangelical Church of Congo is today a member of the World Communion of Reformed Churches and is organized into presbyteries. With roots in Scandinavian Pietism, it has a recognizable Protestant pedigree, but it is not classically Protestant. It has no official confessional statement, and its charismatic and mystical inclinations resemble those of other global Pentecostal movements. As with most charismatics and Pentecostals, the Congolese church recontextualizes distinctly Protestant doctrines like justification by faith alone within a holistic theology of healing and restoration.[6] It is classified as "Protestant" mainly because

---

5. Ibid.

6. The classic statement of this is from William Seymour, one of the leaders of the Azusa Street Revival in 1906. In a seminal article, "Precious Atonement," published in the inaugural issue of *The Apostolic Faith*, Seymour disposed of the normal Protestant emphasis on forgiveness and justification with one line: "Through the atonement we receive forgiveness of sins." The second blessing of the atonement is "sanctification through the blood of Jesus," by which sinners are made sons of God and given authority to rebuke men and demons. Third, Jesus dies for the "healing of our bodies. Sickness and disease are destroyed through the precious atonement of Jesus," Seymour claims, citing Isa 53's promise that "with his stripes we are healed." Atonement is not only for the soul but "for the sanctification of our bodies from inherited disease." The tainted blood inherited by natural birth is cleansed by the blood of Jesus. Finally, the atonement brings "baptism with the Holy Ghost and fire" so that Christ is "enthroned and crowned in our hearts." Jesus is lifted up "in all His fullness, not only in healing and salvation from all sin, but in His power to speak all the languages of the world." The atonement thus includes "justification, sanctification, healing, the baptism with the Holy

it is not Catholic or Orthodox, but that classification depends on the assumption that *every* church *must* fit into one of the three categories. *That* is the assumption we must question. Like many other charismatic/Pentecostal movements, this is really as much a new form of Christianity as the Lutheran or Swiss Reformed churches were novelties in the sixteenth century.

———

Since 1937, thousands have gathered in August every year at a location in Nigeria dubbed "Mount Tabierorar" (also "Tabborrah" or "Taborah") to celebrate a thirteen-day festival of prayer and fasting. The Aladura (Yoruba for "praying people") who celebrate the festival consider it analogous to the biblical festivals at Shiloh, Carmel, or Bashan.[7] About 600,000 attendees from around the world came to the festival in 1991.

Leaders dress in bright red cossack hats and caps. Laymen and -women are robed in stunning white or sky blue, and the women wear headdresses that resemble habits. In vibrant processions, each carries a candle. Choirs sway and clap to the music of brass instruments and drums, singing the Tabieorar anthem:

———

Ghost and signs following." "Precious Atonement" is printed in Vinson Synan and Charles R. Fox, *William J. Seymour: Pioneer of the Azusa Street Revival* (Bridge Logos Foundation, 2012). I am not arguing for a direct connection between Seymour and Kibongi; there seems to be none. But the holism characteristic of African Pentecostalism is analogous to the holism of other charismatic/Pentecostal forms of Christianity.

7. The most extensive description of the festival is found on the Aladura web site, www.aladura.net/tabieorar.htm.

The Mount Tabieorar's Festival has come
Mount Tabieorar is gleeful
The spiritual anniversary has come
Mysterious year has come
All hail the King of Glory
Praise to the Lord of Mercy.

Judged by its costumes, the Tabieorar might be mistaken for a rambunctious African Catholic or Anglican festival, and the impression is strengthened by "high church" aspects of Aladura theology and liturgical practice. Belief in the efficacy of ritual acts is one of the leading features of the church's belief and practice. Aladuras use holy water, prepare liturgical space with incense and candles, perform rites that amount to exorcisms of new automobiles, and believe that their prayers, fasting, and other ritual acts are efficacious when performed in the right place in the right way. Even these "Catholic" features of Aladura, however, are less a product of influence from Western high church traditions than remnants of Yoruba traditional religion.[8]

---

8. See Benjamin C. Ray, "Aladura Christianity: A Yoruba Religion," *Journal of Religion in Africa* 23, no. 3 (1993): 266–91. Though Aladuras sometimes make it sound as if prayer and fasting are "magical," Ray points out that they always acknowledge that God cannot be coerced and *chooses* to answer prayers. In terms made popular by Robin Horton, Aladura shares with traditional Yoruba religion an interest in "explanation, prediction, and control"; see Horton, "African Conversion," *Africa: Journal of International African Institute* 41, no. 2 (1971): 85–108. Christians renounce the means for prediction and control, especially divination, but Aladura Christian has Christian ways to achieve the same ends.

Besides, Aladura has distinctly Protestant features. Beliefs are "based on the principles laid down in the Bible." Aladura Christianity is "biblical in pattern, biblical in the sense that in all matters of faith and conduct, our supreme court of appeal is the Holy Bible."[9] They confess total depravity and justification.

More specifically, Aladura has affinities with African charismatic and Pentecostal movements that are often transplanted from North America, especially in its emphasis on the role of good and evil spirits in everyday social life. One summary of Aladura belief reads in part like the Apostles' Creed (belief in the Trinity of Godhead, Father, Son, and Holy Ghost, the second coming, the final judgment, and an endless new creation), and in part like a charismatic manifesto (belief in divine healing and present-day miracles, baptism of the Spirit, and the gifts of the Spirit).[10] Each year the primate of the Aladura prophesies during the Tabieorar festival.[11] In his 1999 sermon at Tabieorar, Primate Rufus Ositelu expressed the wish that the "God of our forefathers, the God of Tabieorar touch every part of your body, your soul, and every part of your life in Jesus' name." Citing Daniel's encounter with Gabriel and other Scripture

---

9. "The Church of the Lord (Aladura)," *Ecumenical Review* 24, no. 2 (1972): 126.

10. Ibid., 126–27.

11. None is more chilling than Rufus Ositelu's prophecy about the United States, delivered at the festival in August 2000, a prediction concerning the year 2001: "Pray for forgiveness of sin in order to receive the grace of God not to allow less-powerful nation to wage war against them." Quoted at www.aladura.net/tabieorar.htm, citing *Divine Revelations from the Mount TABIEORAR for the Year 2001* (Ogere: Grace Enterprises, 2001), 21.

passages, he taught that God's touch makes enemies flee, it "can give you success in all your undertakings," it "can give you great ability and skills which you never had," it can "make you fearlessly stand for God" and "cleanse you of all your iniquities and remove all your impediments." It can, in sum, "renew your life entirely."[12]

Aladura does not fit easily into a Protestant-Catholic-Orthodox scheme. It is somewhat Catholic, somewhat Protestant, mostly something else entirely—Pentecostalism with an African flavor. Like the Evangelical Church of Congo, it has roots in a Western missionary church. Its founder, Josiah Olunowo Oshitelu, was an Anglican catechist and teacher when he began to have visions of a great "eye" of God and began denouncing the nominal Christianity that surrounded him. The Anglican mission supervisor told him to desist, and when he refused he was removed from his position. After several years of retreat and training, he began to preach in villages, calling people to repentance and promising healing through holy water. The original movement split into four groups—the Christ Apostolic Church, the Cherubim and Seraphim, the Church of the Lord, and the Celestial Church of Christ. Over the following decades, the Aladura movement spread throughout West Africa, into the United Kingdom, and by the early 1980s had established a church in the Bronx.[13] Aladura groups have formed alliances with American

---

12. Quoted at www.aladura.net/tabieorar.htm.
13. This congregation, led by Mother Marie Cooper, is one of the subjects of Mark R. Gornik's *Word Made Global: Stories of African Christianity in New York City* (Grand Rapids: Eerdmans, 2011).

Pentecostal churches, but the attraction of the movement was largely in its promise of Christianity-for-Africans.[14] Aladura is not a continuation of missionary Christianity but was formed in partial opposition to it. Its birth is not unlike the birth of Protestantism.

Vignettes like this could be multiplied almost indefinitely,[15] but they admittedly cannot *prove* anything.

---

14. See Kofi Johnson, "Aladura: The Search for Authenticity, an Impetus for African Christianity," *Asian Journal of Pentecostal Studies* 14, no. 1 (2011): 149–65.

15. In China, for instance, much of the recent growth of the church took place after missionaries were expelled. Even as missionaries were expelled and missions suppressed, indigenous forms of Christian faith were growing, invisible to the West and to a large extent to the Chinese authorities. The Religious Affairs Bureau was closed down in the 1960s, and when it reopened in the 1980s, the Chinese government discovered that the church had grown rapidly under the pressure of persecution. At the end of World War II, there were 840,000 Christians in China; by 1980, there were more than 5 million. Estimates today vary wildly between the official figures that put the Catholic-Protestant population around 20 million and estimates that go as high as 70 million (Joseph Tse-Hei Lee, "Christianity in Contemporary China: An Update," *Journal of Church and State* 49, no. 2 [2007]: 277–304). Scholars divvy up the church that reemerged after the Cultural Revolution into Protestant and Catholic varieties, but, as in Africa, unclassifiable movements have appeared. Some take over Chinese folk traditions, and in several instances leaders have proclaimed themselves to be messianic figures. Others are in the mainstream of Pentecostalism, holding to Christian orthodoxy with an emphasis on the gifts of the Spirit. It was arguably the "radicalism" of Pentecostal Christians that enabled them to endure the horrors of the communist regime. It certainly kept them at some distance from the missionary establishment

even before the missionaries were driven out. Pentecostal experience was intense. Grant Wacker has written of "China's Homegrown Protestants": "At one time or another their religious practices involved diverse manifestations of what social scientists call involuntary motor behavior: weeping, trance-inducing, screaming, howling, numbness, glossolalia, weightlessness, shivering, miraculous healings, profuse sweating, rolling on the floor, frothing at the mouth, ecstatic singing and dancing and extended fasting (in one case, for 76 days). It also involved diverse manifestations of demanding disciplinary rituals such as tithing, exorcisms, foot washing, mass public confessions and communal sharing of goods. The theology paralleled the most severe forms of American Protestant fundamentalism. It entailed conversion, biblical literalism, missions to unconverted Chinese, attempts to evangelize other Christian sects (especially Seventh-day Adventists) and fierce denunciation of mainline Christianity and liberal theology. Millenarianism constituted the most conspicuous feature of this radical Protestant theology. Though the details varied from sect to sect, all of them foresaw the imminent end of history in which the Lord would return in glory, smite his (and, not incidentally, their) enemies and establish a millennial kingdom of peace, justice and prosperity" (Wacker, "China's Homegrown Protestants," *Christian Century* [February 6, 2013]: 32). Wacker is reviewing Lian Xi's *Redeemed by Fire: The Rise of Popular Christianity in Modern China* (New Haven, CT: Yale University Press, 2010). Daniel Bays claims that "a clear majority of rural churches" after 1980, in the places where the church was growing most rapidly, were "quasi-Pentecostal" in "style" (Bays, *A New History of Christianity in China* [London: Wiley Blackwell, 2011], 194). Sunquist too claims that many Chinese churches are "Spirit churches" (*Understanding Christian Mission*, 165). Traditional Protestant denominations continue to have an important presence in China; see, for example, Bruce P. Baugus, ed., *China's Reforming Churches: Mission, Polity, and Ministry in the Next Christendom* (Grand Rapids: Reformation Heritage Books, 2014). These churches are certainly not Orthodox or Catholic, but neither are they entirely Protestant. Indeed, some of the extremer groups denounce the mainstream Three-Self churches as

Whatever they lack in probative force, they possess some power of suggestion, enough to illustrate my initial conclusion: The triad that we have used to map world Christianity has been exploded by the rise of indigenous movements in Africa, and also in Asia and Latin America. These groups have stronger or weaker historic ties with European and North American churches. Many of the prophets of Africa started their life working alongside—or *for*—missionary agencies. They have a family resemblance to Western/Northern churches; despite deviations, many of these movements confess historic Christian beliefs about the Trinity and Christology. But whatever their original relations with the "parent" churches, they have grown up and left home.

Classical Pentecostal churches congealed into denominational structures and are often classified as Protestant. The charismatic movement crossed traditional denominational and national boundaries, but the common dual designations "charismatic Catholic" and "charismatic Episcopal" indicate that the denominational classification was still operative. This was always a distortion. Even in its earliest forms, Pentecostalism was pushing against the borders of the tripartite classification system. Charismatically inflected African Independent Churches and the movements coming out

---

antichrist, much as the Reformers did with the Roman church (Bays, *New History*, 195). As in Africa, these Chinese movements and churches have roots in Western missions, but the trajectory of their expansion and development has been set not by Confessions or a magisterium but by factors that are specifically Chinese.

of Asia have pushed the boundaries further, so that the framework itself is no longer viable.[16] We might group them together as "Spirit churches" or "indigenous churches," but even that scheme distorts as much as it clarifies. Better, we should simply acknowledge that our old maps are as out of date as world maps that show "Yugoslavia" but not "Uzbekistan."[17] We should keep the old maps in a file out of sheer historical interest, but we would be foolish to use the old maps to navigate the world as it is.

The proliferation of independent churches complicates the call of catholicity in a number of ways. It will not do to assume that every church that calls itself Christian is in fact Christian. Some movements in Africa (as well as in Asia and Latin America) have abandoned fundamentals of Christian faith—adherence to Scripture or confession of God as Father, Son, and Spirit—and are not Christian. Many of these new movements renounce written creeds in principle, making

---

16. This needs to be qualified because some of these movements are directly inspired by movements that began in the United States. For an example, see the account of contacts between Ernest Angley and Zambian churches in Paul Gifford, *African Christianity: Its Public Role* (Bloomington: Indiana University Press, 1998), 202-3.

17. Sunquist (*Understanding Christian Mission*, 126) uses the phrase "Spirit churches" and defines them as "churches that identify themselves as led by the Spirit rather than schisms from the sixteenth century (Protestant churches), centered in Rome (Roman Catholic Church), or following a theology from the early church councils (Orthodox)." While these churches testify to "the success of Western missionary work," many were formed in express opposition to missionary churches rather than as continuations of them.

it difficult to sort out which are purveying truth and which are preaching a false gospel. Obviously, the effort to come to one mind and confession, washed by one baptism to eat at one table, is more difficult when we are dealing with several *hundred* potential table companions rather than three. At the same time, the proliferation of varieties of Christianity reconfigures the church and provides an opportunity to approximate more closely the unity that Jesus prays for. A church like the Church of the Lord (Aladura) breaks out of the mold of our current groupings and represents an intersection of Protestant, Catholic, and Pentecostal interests and emphases. Attending to—studying and learning from—these churches may enable Protestant, Catholic, and Orthodox churches to find some common ground beyond our historic barricades.

———

And the opportunity is not "out there" in China or Western Africa. For Americans (also Europeans and Australians), the opportunity is down the street and around the corner.

Global migration has exploded over the past fifty years. In 1960, 76 million people migrated across a national boundary and stayed in the new country for more than a year. The number for 2005 was 191 million, and by 2007 the figure was at 200 million, fully 3 percent of the world's population.[18] North America has a history

---

18. Helen Rose Ebaugh, "Transnationality and Religion in Immigrant Congregations: The Global Impact," *Nordic Journal of Religion and Society* 23, no. 2 (2010): 111.

of receiving migrants, but this is new. Unlike previous waves, the new migration comes not from Europe but from Asia, Africa, and Latin America.[19] Often spurred by political turmoil and economic deprivation in their home countries, thousands of Africans have migrated to North America and Western Europe. More than 10,000 have settled in Belgium. More than half of the new Pentecostal churches planted in London between 2005 and 2012 were black majority churches. Between 2009 and 2014, the Redeemed Church of God started nearly 300 new churches in the United Kingdom.[20] Between 1900 and 1950, around 600 Africans came to the United States each year, but African migration has increased dramatically since immigration laws were adjusted in the early 1960s. Jehu Hanciles writes, "By 2003, African immigrants accounted for 7 percent of all immigrants admitted to the United States. ... In 2002 alone, when the volume of African immigration reached a record high,

---

19. Chinese immigrants living in the US nearly doubled between 1980 and 1990, from 299,000 to 536,000 (Kate Hooper and Jeanne Batalova, "Chinese Immigrants in the United States," *Migration Policy Institute*, January 29, 2015, www.migrationpolicy.org/article/chinese-immigrants-united-states). In the year 2000 it was estimated that there were 200,000 Chinese nationals in Europe (Frank Laczko, "Europe Attracts More Migrants from China," *Migration Policy Institute*, July 1, 2003, www.migrationpolicy.org/article/europe-attracts-more-migrants-china).

20. Ruth Gledhill, "Church Attendance Has Been Propped Up by Immigrants, Says Study," theguardian.com, June 2, 2014, www.theguardian.com/world/2014/jun/03/church-attendance-propped-immigrants-study.

60,269 Africans were admitted into the United States."[21] Specific numbers are hard to come by, but judging by country of origin, many of the migrants to the United States come as Christians. Most of the African immigrants come from Christian rather than Muslim areas

---

21. Jehu Hanciles, *Beyond Christendom: Globalization, African Migration, and the Transformation of the West* (Maryknoll, NY: Orbis, 2008), 306–7. I am focusing on African migrants, but similar movements are evident among Chinese, Hispanics, and Koreans: "According to the best available estimates, there are over 3,500 Catholic parishes [in the US] where Mass is celebrated in Spanish, and 7,000 Hispanic/Latino Protestant congregation, most of them Pentecostal or Evangelical churches, and many of them nondenominational. ... In 1988, the last count available, there were 2,018 Korean-American churches in the United States" (Fenggang Yang and Helen Rose Ebaugh, "Transformations in New Immigrant Religions and their Global Implications," *American Sociological Review* 66, no. 2 [2002]: 271). Already in 1998 there were 700 Chinese Protestant churches in the US (Hanciles, *Beyond Christendom*, 297), and there are Chinese congregations in nearly every state. More than 300 Chinese congregations exist in Canada, Chinese church leaders meet every month in the cross-denominational Greater Vancouver Chinese Ministerial, and there is a similar group in Toronto (Bruce L. Guenther, "Ethnicity and Evangelical Protestants in Canada," in Paul Bramadat and David Seljak, *Christianity and Ethnicity in Canada* [Toronto: University of Toronto Press, 2008], 379–80). We can only imagine what kind of chemical reaction—religious, political, economic—is going to be catalyzed by the growing Chinese presence in sub-Saharan Africa (Howard French, *China's Second Continent: How a Million Migrants Are Building a New Empire in Africa* [New York: Vintage, 2015]).

of Africa.[22] Many become Christians after arriving in the States.[23]

One need not don a pith helmet and board a steamer to find these brothers and sisters. They are living in every major city in the world. They are our neighbors.

It is not clear what effect this new migration will have on the shape of American Christianity in particular. The experience of African churches within Africa does not encourage much hope that the African churches will break down denominational boundaries or encourage greater union among American churches. Catholic-Protestant relations vary from country to country in Africa, and many African churches are as full of vicious, petty conflict as your average American denomination. In the mid-1990s, the Baptist Mission of Zambia was locked in a legal wrangle with the Southern Baptist Conference–related Baptist Convention of Zambia over property.[24] Ecumenical efforts like the United Church of Zambia are rare on the continent.[25] African churches are often led by strong and charismatic church planters who, whatever their intentions, can foster personality cults. At times those tendencies get transferred along with the migrants.

---

22. Hanciles, *Beyond Christendom*, 324.

23. Ibid., 297, notes the disparity between the percentage of Christians in South Korea, Taiwan, and China and the large proportion of Christians among migrants. For example, "only 2 percent of the Taiwanese population is Christian; yet 25 to 30 percent of Taiwanese immigrants in the United States are Christians, and as many as two-thirds of the members of the Taiwanese Christian congregations are converts."

24. Paul Gifford, *African* Christianity, 221.

25. Ibid., 183, 307.

When they come to the States, Africans often have little contact with other American churches, including African American churches. Despite their common heritage and similar liturgical and musical instincts, African and African American Christians live in different worlds. Coming from majority-black cultures, Africans do not grasp the effect of racial prejudices on African Americans and so do not share their sensitivities. Africans are the most highly educated immigrant group, more highly educated on average even than Americans themselves, and they often migrate because of their professional training and skills. With high levels of education and professional achievement, they are separated socially and economically from many American blacks, whom they sometimes regard as lazy and whiny. Africans are aghast at the breakdown of family life among African Americans, the high rates of illegitimacy, single parenthood, and teen pregnancy. Africans accept many of the stereotypes that American whites have of African Americans and are regarded with some suspicion by American blacks.[26]

At their best, African immigrant churches represent missionary efforts from Africa to the developed world. Africans sometimes migrate with the specific aim of evangelizing and ministering in the increasingly secularized United States. Darlingston Johnson was visiting America in 1990 when his native Liberia fell apart. Making a virtue of necessity, he determined that he had been exiled to start a mission. According to Johnson, God told him, "Don't be refugees, be missionaries."

---

26. Hanciles, *Beyond Christendom*, 320–21.

The Bethel World Outreach Church that he started in Silver Springs, Maryland, in 1990 now has several thousand members and is the flagship church for a global network of 150 churches. Many African migrant churches aspire, like Johnson's, to be more than an ethnic enclave for West Africans. Forty-two nations are represented in Bethel's Silver Springs congregation.[27] Not all churches are so successful in attracting non-African members. Despite his best efforts, Oladipo Kalejaiye's International Christian Center in Los Angeles is still a majority Nigerian congregation.[28]

It is possible that African churches will go the way of European immigrant churches—first serving as ethnic outposts, gradually slipping into the mainstream as yet another eddy in the river of American Christianity. Insofar as American denominationalism is rooted in ethnic identity, the African immigrant churches may simply reinforce American denominationalism and so add to the fragmentation of the American church. In the long run, African migrant churches may provide another piece of evidence for the social sources of American denominationalism and the continuing failure of the church to be the church embracing people of every tongue, people, and nation.[29]

---

27. Ibid., 328–33.

28. Hanciles, *Beyond Christendom*, 337. As Peggy Levitt makes clear, not every Christian option in the States originated in the States. See Levitt, *God Needs No Passport: Immigrants and the Changing American Religious Landscape* (New York: New Press, 2007).

29. The classic study of the social origins of American denominationalism is H. Richard Niebuhr, *The Social Sources of Denominationalism* (New York: Henry Holt, 1929).

Denominationalism is, however a mixed curse. While denominations often replicate worldly ethnic, economic, national, and racial distinctions, the very fact of religious diversity creates a certain amount of pressure toward forms of interdenominational recognition and cooperation. In a study of thirteen immigrant religious institutions in Houston, Texas, Fenggang Yang and Helen Rose Ebaugh discovered that various factors pressured the groups simultaneously toward a form of "ecumenism" and toward a form of "fundamentalism." Buddhism, for instance, is divided into subtraditions that follow the geographic distribution of Buddhism. Mahayana Buddhism dominates China, Korea, Japan, and Korea, while Theravada Buddhism is concentrated in Southeast Asia. In Houston, Buddhists of different traditions encounter one another, sometimes for the first time, and they "check out" Buddhist temples from other countries: "Regular attendees at the Chinese Mahayana His Nan Temple include people from Burma, India, Sri Lanka, Thailand, and Vietnam." A Houston Buddhist Council has arisen from these international, "ecumenical" contacts.[30]

This cross-ethnic, cross-tradition contact also creates pressure toward what Yang and Ebaugh call "fundamentalism." Despite their differences in thought and practice, Mahayana Buddhists regard Theravada Buddhists as adherents of the same religion, but to determine what they share, they reach "back to the original founder and/or some historic, authoritative leaders of the religion, and to the commonly recognized holy

---

30. Yang and Ebaugh, "Transformations," 279.

scriptures."[31] They discover a basic, common "creed" that unites them despite their differences. Yang and Ebaugh discovered similar catholicizing pressures on Christian immigrant groups. Third-generation

> Greek Americans in our Houston study ... favor a pan-orthodox Christian Church that would unite many ethnic orthodox churches that now exist. ... By emphasizing common origins, doctrines, and rituals, the pan-orthodox supporters favor the establishment of a united Orthodox church in order to increase the visibility and the religious, economic, and political power of Eastern orthodoxy in America as well as to emphasize unity among believers.[32]

Immigrants, further, do not keep their new religious experiences and insights to themselves. Whatever happens in Vegas, the experience of American Buddhists does not stay in America. Because many recent migrants are "transnational"—maintaining close ties with their home country while living in, and even becoming a citizens of, another country—they export fresh ideas and religious perspectives back to the home country. Buddhist "ecumenism" spreads from the States back to China and Sri Lanka. Similarly, the experiences of Christian immigrants in their encounters with the variety of Christian options in America could inspire ecumenical efforts back home. African immigrant churches might, for instance, encounter varied forms of American

31. Ibid.
32. Ibid., 279–80.

Christianity that would lead them to a form of "ecumenical fundamentalism" exportable back to the African context. An ecumenism inspired by Greek Orthodox in America could have an impact on Orthodoxy back home in Greece, the Balkans, and Russia.

New ethnic churches have contributed to a "de-Europeanization" of American Christianity. Immigrants often

> come from Latin American origins that are predominantly Christian, such as Mexico, Puerto Rico, the Dominican Republic, Cuba, Haiti, El Salvador, and Guatemala. Filipinos (the second largest Asia-origin immigrant group) are predominantly Christian as well. While Christianity is a minority religion in Korea, Vietnam, and India, there has been selective immigration by Christians from those countries.[33]

In Europe, large Muslim migrant populations have furthered "de-Christianization" (though even in Europe, that is not the whole story), but in the United States there has been no de-Christanization. On the contrary, Christianity has been revitalized by immigrants. Roman Catholic immigrants from Latin America have saved American Catholicism, and Protestant churches have benefitted from the influx of committed, vibrant believers from Latin America, Asia, and Africa.[34] Insofar as divisions of the American church are the product of battles fought in Europe, the de-Europeanization

---

33. Ibid., 271.
34. Hanciles, *Beyond Christendom*, 293–96.

of Christianity in the States may ameliorate some of those divisions.

But there is a deeper, more subtle reason to hope that the new immigrant churches may tilt American Christianity toward unity. To see this, we need to take a longer look at the shape of American denominationalism. H. Richard Niebuhr's claim that denominationalism violates the gospel because it installs ethnic and socioeconomic distinctions within the church is only the most visible and obvious aspect of denominationalism. From another angle, the denominational system produces highly unified, even uniform churches.

In an article as classic as Niebuhr's book, Sidney Mead argues that a denomination is "not primarily confession" or "territorial" but rather "purposive."[35] It is a form of church life symbiotic with a particular political location. A denomination "has no official connection with a civil power whatsoever" but is a "voluntary association of like-hearted and like-minded individuals, who are united on the basis of common beliefs for the purpose of accomplishing some tangible and defined objectives."[36] This situation has produced a distinctive pattern of churchmanship, which Mead summarizes under six heads: (1) A denominational church has a "sectarian" tendency to "justify its peculiar interpretations and practices as more closely conforming to those of the early Church as pictured in the New Testament

---

35. Sidney Mead, "Denominationalism: The Shape of Protestantism in America," reprinted in Russell E. Richey, ed., *Denominationalism* (Eugene, OR: Wipf & Stock [1977] 2010), 70–105.
36. Ibid., 71.

than the views and politics of its rivals"; (2) denominations are based on a voluntary principle and depend on persuasion rather than coercion; (3) denominations are missionary organizations, and this mission-mindedness has accounted too for the "interdenominational or superdenominational consciousness and cooperation which has been such an outstanding aspect of the American religious life"; (4) denominations are revivalist; (5) in America, many denominations have defined themselves in opposition to Enlightenment Reason, while paradoxically accepting the parameters of a church-state settlement rooted in Enlightenment reason; (6) finally, denominational churches are competitive institutions in a religious free market.[37]

American denominationalism's "voluntaryism" works against deep theology. Denominations are defined by activity more than theology, and Mead thinks this encourages the idea that Christian faith itself is "an activity, a movement, which the group is engaged in promoting." This setting encourages the formation of certain kinds of leaders, and not ones who are profound theologians: "Whatever else top denominational leaders may be, they *must* be denominational politicians."[38] Voluntaryism has political consequences too. American churches accept the American settlement of religious freedom, and that implies that "only what all the religious 'sects' held and taught in common ... was really relevant for the well being of the society and the state." Americans need to be religious, but (to paraphrase

---

37. Ibid., 75–102.
38. Ibid., 81–83.

Eisenhower) it does not matter what religion it is, so long as it maintains publicly useful tenets—like religious freedom. Conversely, "the churches implicitly accepted the view that whatever any religious group held peculiarly as a tenet of its faith, must be irrelevant for public welfare." American churches teach their distinctive doctrines and views, and so divide themselves from each other, but those things that justify the existence of the denomination are "either irrelevant for the general welfare or at most possessed only a kind of instrumental value for it."

America's denominational churches, in short, have implicitly agreed that they will subordinate their public witness to the generic faith of American civil religion. Denominationalism is not *dis*establishment but the form that Protestant *establishment* has taken in the United States.[39]

---

39. Fred J. Hood's study of the "evolution" of denominationalism among the Reformed churches of the Mid-Atlantic and Southern states ("Evolution of the Denomination among the Reformed of the Middle and Southern States, 1780–1840," in Richey, ed., *Denominationalism*) is highly illuminating on this and other points. Early on denominations were understood as having to do with the internal government of the church. Missions, and especially the patriotic mission of Christianizing America, was carried out not through denominational structures but through the myriad voluntary societies that came into existence in the early nineteenth century: "In the wake of the fragmentation of Protestantism and the retreat of civil government from jurisdiction in matters of religion, the societies seemed to be the most efficient way to encourage religion and therefore promote the national welfare" (148). These societies claimed to be, and in some ways were, ecumenical efforts, but Hood argues that most of them were guided by some sectarian vision. The American Sunday School Union

African migrant churches have the potential to subvert this denominational system in several ways. Though Africans, like most immigrants, come to the States with hopes for economic betterment, they are not participants in the mythologies of American liberal order. In some African countries, churches are deeply embedded in the life of the nations. For all its ambiguities and failures, the 1991 declaration of Zambia as a Christian nation indicated that African Christians are not necessarily adopting the liberal politics of the modern West.[40] African Christians seem instinctively aware that politics cannot be religiously neutral, that political struggles are always also spiritual struggles. African migrant churches come to America with an implicit political theology sharply at odds with Americanism, and sharply at odds with the denominationalism that is the ecclesial face of Americanism.

The transnationality of the African churches also works against the civil religion that permeates American denominationalism. During the nineteenth

---

was controlled by middle-state and Southern Reformed churches, and the United Domestic Missionary Society was primarily funded and manned by Reformed groups (153).

40. For details of the hypocrisies involved and the controversies the declaration provoked, see Gifford, *African Christianity*, 197–219. At the time President Chiluba said, "On behalf of the nation. I have now entered into covenant with the living God. ... I submit the Government and the entire nation of Zambia to the Lordship of Jesus Christ. I further declare that Zambia is a Christian nation that will seek to be governed by the righteous principles of the Word of God" (quoted in Gifford, 198). These are words that have not been uttered by a Western political leader since the seventeenth century.

century, American Protestants regarded Catholic immigrants with suspicion because they were "subjects" of a sovereign other than the United States—the pope in the Vatican. Though the suspicion was an expression of ignorant anti-Catholicism and nativist prejudice, the Protestants were not entirely wrong. Catholics *did* identify with a "foreign power," an international religious communion that was not under the control of the American government. Protestant immigrants had a long tradition of subordinating religious aims to national policy and therefore were considered safe for America.

Though some African immigrant churches had their origins in the States, those following what Jehu Hanciles calls the "Macedonian model" were deliberately planted by Africa-based churches. The Church of Pentecost, based in Ghana, now has a US branch with 70 local "assemblies" and more than 10,000 members. The Nigerian Redeemed Church of God has 175 churches in the US and also has more than 10,000 members.[41] The Anglican Mission in America is a variation on this theme—a collection of Anglican congregations in the United States ruled by the Anglican bishop of Rwanda. These churches weaken American denominationalism insofar as they are part of networks that extend beyond American borders and are not beholden to the American civil religion. And by weakening American

---

41. Hanciles, *Beyond Christendom*, 350–56.

denominationalism, they open up the prospect of bridg-
ing denominational divides.[42]

———

This is not automatic by any means. The slow, partial Americanization of the Catholic Church suggests
that African migrant churches might well become as
American as any other church, adapting over the generations to the American order, American civil religion,
and the denominational system. Here technology may
serve the interests of catholicity: Africans can remain
rooted in their home countries more easily because of
advances in travel and communications technologies.
It is possible today, as it was not during the nineteenth

———

42. Peggy Levitt has made a similar argument with respect to
Latinos in the US. Since, she writes, "we live in an increasingly differentiated society," Latinos bring "their own versions of
Judeo-Christian norms and practices that may challenge the ex-
isting value consensus." This means that "America's civil religious
fabric is being irrevocably rewoven in the process of incorporat-
ing new Latino immigrants" since "civil religion no longer stops
are our borders but, rather, that increasingly it is a set of values
and beliefs that is transnationally defined" ("Two Nations under
God? Latino Religious Life in the United States," in Marcelo M.
Suarez-Orozco and Mariela Paez, eds., *Latinos: Remaking America*
[Berkeley: University of California Press, 2002], 161). Levitt attri-
butes this in part to the role of John Paul II in forming a "global
civil society" (the phrase is from Jose Casanova), a "vision of community in which nation-state boundaries recede and a religious
transnational civil society takes center stage. He offers an alternative membership that also empowers, protects, and speaks out
for its members" (158). See Levitt's discussion of "religious global
citizens" as critical examples of cosmopolitan globalization (*God
Needs No Passport*, 83–88).

century, for a bishop in Rwanda to oversee churches in the United States.

Besides, we might, out of fear, envy, or self-protective pride, blow it. Mark Gornik worries that, faced with unclassifiable new Christian movements, Western churches might "seek to protect or even try to establish its position as normative" or "to acknowledge other viewpoints but ignore any deep engagement."[43] It has happened before, among missionaries who either ignored or denounced indigenous Christian movements, without any real effort to listen, engage, or understand them. Dean Gilliland spent two decades as a missionary with the United Methodist Church in Nigeria. He confessed that for the first decade and a half, he paid no attention to the African Independent Churches, except to denounce: "I considered it my Christian responsibility to warn all pastors and interested laymen against them," since he considered them "heretical" and even "satanic." Churches transplanted from Europe and North America were ignorant of the goings-on in these exotic communities, and what little they knew scared them.[44] Gilliland's experience was not unique. Some churches enter the mission field to advance their own theological tradition, sometimes in competition with other Western churches: Presbyterians who need to win Asia for Presbyterianism, Anglicans who want an Anglican

---

43. Gornik, *Word Made Global*, 266–67.
44. Dean Gilliland, "How 'Christian' Are African Independent Churches?" *Missiology* 14, no. 3 (1986): 259–72. The divide was not merely between missionary and indigenous churches. The independent churches themselves have little connection with one another, sometimes because of a history of schism and battle.

Africa. As a result, Western conflicts are globalized. The gospel is preached, people convert, but it is a great waste of energy and talent. For the point, obviously, is to win the world for Jesus, not for any denomination. When that point is lost, denominations cease to be denominations and become schismatic sects.

Above I used "grown up" advisedly, and that phrase nudges the discussion in a more practical direction. Leave aside questions about the legitimacy of Western missionary "paternalism" in the nineteenth century. It is past time for first-world Christians to acknowledge that in dealing with Aladura believers or members of the Redeemed Church of God, we are dealing with *brothers*, from whom we may learn at least as much as we can teach. A handful of majority-world Evangelicals have been recognized as theological peers, not only explaining their traditions to the rest of us but making constructive contributions to evangelical theology. Simon Chan, who teaches at Trinity Theological College in Singapore, has written on Pentecostal theology, but his *Liturgical Theology* (InterVarsity Press, 2009) contributes to the renewal of interest in liturgy among evangelicals. Amos Yong has been president of the Society for Pentecostal Studies, but he has the stature to offer a meditation on the future of evangelical theology from an Asian American, Pentecostal perspective. Ugandan Catholic Emmanuel Katongole writes mainly on Africa and African theology, but he has done so from prominent positions at Duke and Notre Dame.

These figures are the proverbial tip of the iceberg, but more voices from non-Western churches need to be heard. Katongole has complained that "Africa has not become the subject of serious theological inquiry in the United States, or generally in the West." African issues—issues like healing and medicine, miracles and spirits, prophecy and gifts of the Spirit—"remain peripheral to the theological project of the West." Katongole thinks that this negligence could be "disastrous for the future of World Christianity." Without serious theological engagement, clichés about the growing importance of African Christianity will be "hollow."[45] We Westerners should get used to being challenged to revisit our faith when we hear it sung in a new tongue.

Capitalizing on the opportunity will require mortification of old habits and instincts. It will mean seizing what Andrew Walls called the "Ephesian moment," a moment in which the encounter between different Christian traditions involves mutual giving and receiving, mutual listening and learning and teaching, openness among Western believers to the new forms of faith that are emerging from worlds we barely know and certainly do not understand. Only in this way can we reach the fullness of Christ for, as Walls says, "none of us can reach Christ's completeness on our own. We need each other's vision to correct, enlarge and focus our own; only together are we complete in Christ."[46] To exploit the ecumenical potential of denominationalism, Christians will need to get out of their denominational ghettoes.

---

45. Emanuel Katongole, "A Tale of Many Stories," in Darren Marks, ed., *Shaping a Global Theological Mind* (Aldershot, UK: Ashgate, 2008), 89, quoted in Gornik, *Word Made Global*, 264.
46. Andrew F. Walls, *The Cross-Cultural Process in Christian History: Studies in the Transmission and Appropriation of Faith* (Maryknoll, NY: Orbis, 2002), 79.

Pastors and churches that want to pursue global catholicity can start local. Large-scale ecumenical efforts have borne fruit—some nourishing, some rotten—but most pastors will never have the opportunity to engage other churches at that level. That does not prevent them from advancing the unity of the church. It is not rocket science or labor intensive. A few minutes on Google will locate the Chinese or Korean or Kenyan or Somali or Columbian or Ecuadorean churches in your town. Pastors can search out a handful of international pastors who are willing to pray and study Scripture together every week. Churches can find ways to serve and share with immigrant churches by offering language training or by helping to navigate the job or housing markets. European, North American, and Australian churches can experience Pentecost all over again by worshiping with churches from various tribes, tongues, nations, and peoples.

God is changing the maps, and we are simply called to follow the one Lord of the one church.

SCRIPTURE INDEX

Old Testament

New Testament